MW00943908

Love Letters

From God

A daily devotional designed to encourage, uplift, and heighten your union with Christ

Steve Eden

Copyright © 2017 Steve Eden

All rights reserved.

ISBN-13: 978-1977740229

ISBN-10: 1977740227

DEDICATION

I would like to dedicate this book to my three children: Noel, Caleb, and Joshua. May it be a constant reminder to each of you that God's voice is always near, always tender, and always truthful.

From The Author:

It is my prayer and passion that this devotional touches the very deepest places of your heart and walk with Christ. So many of these words from the Lord came during very quiet and worshipful times that drew me ever closer to His faithfulness, His character, and His heart for people just like me. What a wonder to know that God wants to speak lovingly and openly with His children! The enemy has tried to use fear, failure, and religion to conceal our Heavenly Father's desire to communicate with us. My hope is that this book empowers you to know your Father's voice and to comprehend the greatness of His unrelenting love that came to us through Jesus Christ.

Forever His,

Steve Eden

Love Letters From God

Day 1 - Your Father's Love

"Breathe in My peace and be at rest. Close out the other voices. Sense My Presence around, above, and in you. Have you ever known a greater love? Have you ever known a safer place? Lock eyes with Me and see your Defender and Protector. You want Me to fix what is going on around you; yet I want to fix your attitude and your perspective. Fear is not of Me. Worry is not of Me. My perfect love for you casts out all fear. I am your light, your defense, and your salvation -- of whom shall you be afraid?"

Today's Scriptures:

Psalm 27:1 – *The Lord is my light and my salvation; Whom shall I fear? The Lord is the strength of my life; of whom shall I be afraid?*

1 John 4:18 – *There is no fear in love; but perfect love casts out all fear, because fear involves torment. But he who fears has not been made perfect in love.*

Day 2 - Your Identity

"You are not being made into something else...you already ARE! You may continue to be strengthened and to grow, but you've already received your new identity. You may continue to be sharpened, and you may learn over time how to use all the tools you've been given, but you DO already possess them. Awaken to that reality. Your identity is NOT a work in progress, but a completed masterpiece! The only thing left for you is to discover the intricacies that are already woven into your tapestry."

Today's Scriptures:

2 Corinthians 5:17 – *Therefore, if anyone is in Christ, he is a new creation; old things have passed away; behold, all things have become new.*

Galatians 2:20 – *I have been crucified with Christ; it is no longer I who live, but Christ lives in me.*

Day 3 - Your Divine Design

"Discover the beauty of what has already been created in you. It's all there, and has been there since the very moment you received Me. All along I've known your design. You didn't happen by accident. I didn't make things up as I went along fashioning you. Your mistakes, missteps, and so-called "flaws" didn't influence your creation or place stains or tears in the fabric of who you are. The only thing that influenced your design was My purpose for you. And here you are-- complete, equipped, and in the place and time I set apart for you."

Today's Scriptures:

Psalm 139:13-14 – For You formed my inward parts; You covered me in my mother's womb. [14] I will praise You for I am fearfully and wonderfully made; Marvelous are Your works, and that my soul knows very well.

Colossians 2:10 – You are complete in Christ, who is the head of all principality and power.

Day 4 - Total Forgiveness

"Today I sing a song of forgiveness in your heart. Will you hear Me? How good, pleasant, and liberating to release the debts of others, as well as to forgive one's self, for My forgiveness heals when you get it and when you give it. It is not justifiable for you to hold a grudge when I have provided such complete and total forgiveness for you. Remember, there is nothing I hold between us, nothing -- My blood has cleansed it all."

Today's Scriptures:

Ephesians 1:7 (NIV) – In Him we have redemption through His blood, the forgiveness of sins, in accordance with the riches of His grace.

Ephesians 4:32 – Be kind to one another, tender hearted, forgiving each other even as God in Christ forgave you.

Hebrews 10:14 – For by one offering, Christ has perfected forever those being made holy.

4

Day 5 - Believe The Truth

"My child, listen to Me. Hearken unto My words. You must not center yourself on yourself -- thinking if you do ok, then you're accepted; or thinking if you do ok, then you're righteous. Stop trying and start trusting. Trusting that I am who has made you accepted in the Beloved. Trusting that I have made you a king and a priest. You keep trying to fix your behavior and what you need to do is believe the truth. The truth of who I say you are. The truth of who I made you to be. The truth of your holiness, your call, and your oneness with Me."

Today's Scriptures:

1 Peter 2:9-10 – You are a chosen generation, a royal priesthood, a holy nation, His own special people, that you may proclaim the praises of Him who called you out of darkness into His marvelous light; [10] *you once were not a people but are now the people of God, who had not obtained mercy but now have obtained mercy.*

Day 6 - The Father's Plans

"Do not look to yourself but look to the truth that already exists in Me. It's your only hope for the quiet strength and success you seek. Do not over complicate matters. You don't have to solve everything. Trust in Me. Trust in My finished work. Yes, I know you have problems. Yes, I know you're not perfect outwardly, but I will complete the work I've begun in you if you will but walk humbly with Me and center everything on Me. I am proud of you. I have not given up on you. I have plans for you. Plans for a future and a hope. Plans of us walking hand in hand fulfilling the Father's purposes."

Today's Scriptures:

Jeremiah 29:11 – For I know the thoughts that I think toward you, says the Lord, thoughts of peace and not of evil, to give you a future and a hope.

Proverbs 3:5 – Trust in the Lord with all your heart, lean not on your own understanding.

Day 7 - Made For God

"My precious child, embrace and recall our story each and every day. For when you took My yoke, you found it easy. When you accepted My love, you found it healing. When you received My grace, you found it empowering. And of course with certainty – when you found Me, you found yourself. You found your meaning, your purpose, your value, and your destiny. We belong together because I made you for Myself, Me in you and you in Me, forever as One."

Today's Scriptures:

Matthew 11:28-30 – *"Come to Me, all you who labor and are heavy laden, and I will give you rest. 29 Take My yoke upon you and learn from Me, for I am gentle and lowly in heart, and you will find rest for your souls. 30 For My yoke is easy and My burden is light."*

Colossians 1:16 – *All things were created by Him and for Him.*

Day 8 - Made For Forgiveness

"It is not healthy or beneficial to harbor resentments because you are made in My image and I am not a resentful God. There is nothing more unnatural, unhealthy, and unsatisfying than harboring ill will. For the enemy says it gives you power over others, when in fact he uses it to take power over you. So hear My heart inside your heart today – My forgiveness came TO you so I could then get it THROUGH you."

Today's Scriptures:

Colossians 3:12-13 – Therefore, as the elect of God, holy and beloved, put on tender mercies, kindness, humility, meekness, patience; [13] bearing with one another, and forgiving one another, if anyone has a complaint against another; even as Christ forgave you.

Matthew 18:33 – "Should you not have had mercy on your fellow servant just as I had mercy on you?"

Day 9 - Do Not Worry

"Do not worry about your future, I am already there. Do not worry about your past, I have already cleansed it. Do not worry about your present for My presence is already with you and in you. Therefore, rise and lead. Be confident and unwavering. No need to hide your weaknesses from Me, I see them and will love and lead you through them as I have always promised. You are fully known and fully loved and I am fully committed to your growth and development."

Today's Scriptures:

Matthew 6:25-26 – *'I say to you, do not be worried about your life, as to what you will eat or drink; or wear.* ^{26} *Look at the birds of the air, that they do not sow, nor reap nor gather into barns, and yet your heavenly Father feeds them. Are you not worth much more than they?'*

Philippians 4:6 (NLT) – *Don't worry about anything; instead, pray about everything. Tell God your need and thank him for all He's done.*

Day 10 - Righteousness Matters

"Welcome back My child. Transfixed by the natural? I tell you truly you are one in a million. I handcrafted you in your mother's womb. You are significant. Today we walk in righteousness because righteousness matters - just not for the reasons religion taught you. Righteousness matters because of love. Righteousness matters because you should not cast your pearls before swine, lest people turn and tear you to pieces. Righteousness matters because while the world cannot discredit My message, they will try to discredit My messengers, and you are truly one of My finest. Welcome back."

Today's Scriptures:

Matthew 7:6 – *"Do not give what is holy to the dogs; nor cast your pearls before swine, lest they trample them under their feet, and turn and tear you in pieces."*

Romans 13:10 – *Love does no harm to its neighbor therefore love is the fulfillment of the law.*

Day 11 - God's Idea

"Strength and might are yours as I am moving you deeper into faith. I am making you more comfortable believing all I say about you. For example: I created you so I could be with you. It's ok to believe it, it was My idea. I redeemed you with My Son's precious blood. It's ok to believe it, it was My idea. I made you righteous and clean. It's ok to believe it, it was My idea. I made you adequate and complete in Me. It's ok to believe that too, it was My idea. When the time was just right, when the world needed your gifts, I opened eternity and formed you in your mother's womb. It's ok to believe all I've done for you, it was ALL My idea."

Today's Scriptures:

1 Peter 1:18-19 – Knowing that you were not redeemed with corruptible things, like silver or gold, from your aimless conduct received by tradition from your fathers, ¹⁹ but with the precious blood of Christ, as of a lamb without blemish and without spot.

Day 12 - Receive of God

"Like a child, if you can receive you can live. Do not stress or strain to love, but love with the love I have given you. Do not stress or strain to forgive, but forgive with the forgiveness I have already supplied you. You cannot give away what you have not first taken the time to receive from Me because receiving always precedes producing. And with that - what good thing have I withheld from you? I tell you no good thing, for all My love is yours, all My mercy is yours, all My kindness is yours; and not because you're so faithful but because I am."

Today's Scriptures:

1 John 4:19-20 – We love Him because He first loved us. [20] If someone says, "I love God," and hates his brother, he is a liar; for he who does not love his brother whom he has seen, how can he love God whom he has not seen?

Day 13 - Believe The Truth

"Rise and rise again. Your circumstances have no power over you. What others say or do does not control your demeanor. I am on the throne of your heart, not them; and I am the greater One. I am the ruling One. I have not only captured your heart but filled it with My Spirit and My love. It is written, "Greater is He that is within you than He that is in the world." That is the truth. Your believing it does not make it true, your believing it allows you to experience the life and freedom of it. Live the truth. Know the truth. It not only sets you free, it keeps you in the reality of your freedom!"

Today's Scriptures:

1 John 4:4 – You are of God, little children, and have overcome them, because He who is in you is greater than he who is in the world.

Ephesians 2:10 (NIV) – For we are God's handiwork, created in Christ Jesus to do good works, which God prepared in advance for us to do.

Day 14 - Your Identity

"Peace, be still. Let Me speak words of life over you. You are loved unconditionally. You are My beloved child, chosen by Me for good works. You are divinely anointed and appointed for such a time as this. You are complete in Me. You are adequate in Me. You are My ambassador. You are marked by Me and made by Me for: peace, love, joy, humility, kindness, gentleness, and self-control. Let Me be your source and no other, for I am good. I not only mean well, I mean you well."

Today's Scriptures:

2 Corinthians 5:20 – Now then, we are ambassadors for Christ, as though God were pleading through us: we implore you on Christ's behalf, be reconciled to God.

Romans 8:14 – For as many as are led by the Spirit of God, these are the sons of God.

Day 15 - Your Father's Love

"From before there was time, I have loved you. And no, I don't even have to work hard at it. It's easy for Me to love you because I know you. Embrace My unfailing love—it strengthens and empowers you. Nobody else knows you like I know you; not even you. And I believe in you. I know the good I have put in you in Christ. Close out those old negative voices and trust Me instead. Trust My process. Trust My Spirit who WILL complete the work I've began in you."

Today's Scriptures:

1 John 3:16 – *By this we know love, because He laid down His life for us. And we also ought to lay down our lives for the brethren.*

Philemon 1:6 – *That the sharing of your faith may become effective by the acknowledgment of every good thing which is in you in Christ Jesus.*

Day 16 - Your Calling

"Emerge into this new season with joy. Old things have passed away, behold new things have come. It's time to press on towards your high calling; to lay hold of that for which I laid hold of you. It's time to forget what is behind, and to reach forward to what is ahead. I have not brought you this far to let you go or to see you overtaken. There is nothing you will face outside of you greater than Who is inside of you. Dare to believe My healing hand is with you and My loving hand guides you. Hold fast to the truth --not the truth of the world, but the truth I've placed deep in your inner man!"

Today's Scriptures:

Philippians 3:12-13 – Not that I have already attained, or am already perfected; but I press on, that I may lay hold of that for which Christ has also laid hold of me. ¹³ I do not count myself to have apprehended; but one thing I do, forgetting those things that are behind I reach forward to those things which are ahead.

Day 17 - Preeminent Christ

"I didn't send My Son to begin man's search for God, I sent Him to end it. Religion is man's search for Me but Christ is My search for man. No one has to work hard to find Me, I am ever watching and waiting -- all they have to do is turn around, yield inwardly, and they'll be immediately in the arms of redemptive love. My Son is the preeminent One, the radiance of My glory, and the embodiment of My true nature. Look upon Him and live."

Today's Scriptures:

Hebrews 1:3 (GWT) – *His Son is the reflection of God's glory and the exact likeness of God's being. He holds everything together through His powerful words. After He had cleansed people from their sins, He now holds the honored position—the one next to the majestic God [the Father] on the heavenly throne.*

John 1:18 (GWT) – *No one has ever seen God. God's only Son, the One who is closest to the Father's heart, has made him known.*

Day 18 - Rise Again

"Trust and be not afraid. Have I not brought you this far? I tell you truly I have. I am aware you don't always choose right, but My grace is sufficient for you. Live the life I have given you to live. Express the love and sincerity I have given you to express. Do not walk in self-protection or fear, those are not of Me. My gift to you is innocence, a pure heart, a clear conscience, and freedom in and by and through My Spirit. Even though you may stumble, rise and rise and rise again."

Today's Scriptures:

Proverbs 24:16 (GWT) – *A righteous person may fall seven times, but he gets up again.*

2 Corinthians 12:9 – *And He said to me, "My grace is sufficient for you, for My strength is made perfect in weakness." Therefore most gladly I will rather boast in my infirmities, that the power of Christ may rest upon me.*

Day 19 - Never Give Up

"Rest in My love with nothing to prove. Rely on Me for your validation and worth. Receive daily of My supply, then you can reflect Me to others. I am patient with you. I am kind. I will never give up on you so never give up on Me. I will get you across the finish line. I will complete the work I've begun in you. I will take what the enemy meant for harm and use it to strengthen you. Stay the course. Stay humble, gentle; always teachable and always willing to learn. Full of mercy and good fruit."

Today's Scriptures:

Philippians 1:6 – Being confident of this very thing, that He who has begun a good work in you will complete it until the day of Jesus Christ.

1 Corinthians 13:4 – Love suffers long and is kind; love does not envy; love does not parade itself, love is not puffed up.

Day 20 - Higher Living

"Break free from old patterns that beset you. When you stumble, quickly remember who you really are and renew your mind to how righteous I've made you. Remember this day how accepted you are, clean you are, and deeply loved you are. You are not an unholy being trying to be holy. You are a blessed new creation learning to walk in the reality of your true identity. Sin and the flesh pull on you like gravity but My Life and Spirit daily beckon you higher. Listen and take heed to My Voice that you may truly live."

Today's Scriptures:

Romans 12:2 – _Do not be conformed to this world, but be transformed by the renewing of your mind, that you may prove what is that good and acceptable and perfect will of God._

Romans 8:2 – _For the law of the Spirit of life in Christ Jesus has made me free from the law of sin and death._

Day 21 - Love Purely

"Arise and awake My child. Love purely and sincerely today without hypocrisy. In honor give preference to others. Be patient in tribulation, continuing steadfastly in prayer. Bless those who persecute you, bless and do not curse. Never let your response to someone's sin be as ugly as what they did to you. Resist pride and self-centeredness; instead do justly, love mercy, and walk humbly with Me. Stay yielded, you shall not be overcome. Bound to Me you walk the earth free!!"

Today's Scriptures:

Micah 6:8 – He has shown you, O man, what is good; And what does the Lord require of you but to do justly, to love mercy, and to walk humbly with your God?

Romans 12:10 – Be kindly affectionate to one another with brotherly love, in honor giving preference to one another.

Day 22 - Your Rescue

"I didn't come to condemn you, I came to rescue you. I didn't come to ostracize you, I came to draw you to Myself. I am not your estrangement, I am your homecoming. Embrace My tender heart towards you and I will change yours. I will take from you a stony heart and give you a heart of flesh. Let Me teach you how to love. Let Me teach you how to forgive. Do you not know I love you into loving and forgive you into forgiving? I rescue you into rescuing others. My heart is big. My love knows no boundaries where you are concerned. I arise with healing in My wings this day, just open up and receive."

Today's Scriptures:

John 3:17 – *"God sent not His Son into the world to condemn the world but that the world through Him might be saved."*

1 Thessalonians 4:9 – *You have no need that I should write you, for you yourselves are taught by God to love one another.*

Day 23 - Brought Near

"My child, rest in Me. Why do you strain and strive as though you're achieving something for Me? You cannot add anything to what I've already done for you. I've brought you near by My own hand, My own blood, through My own heart for you. Be free, knowing you lack for nothing. All that is Mine is yours. You don't need the validation of others, I have already validated you. Stay the course of righteousness, for it is not just My way it is your way. It leads to open doors and Kingdom opportunities."

Today's Scriptures:

John 6:29 – Jesus answered and said to them, "This is the work of God, that you believe in Him whom He sent."

Ephesians 2:13 – But now in Christ Jesus you who once were far off have been brought near by the blood of Christ.

Day 24 - Source For Truth

"Incline your ear to My words, for they are health to your body and peace to your mind. The truest thing about you is what I say about you. Since the day you received Me, I made you clean and holy; complete and forgiven. I know you don't always feel this way, but it is true. Each day assess who or what you are using to determine your value. Assess who is your source for truth. Is it your behavior, your feelings, your thoughts? Is it the opinion of others? They weren't there the day I formed you in your mother's womb. How can anyone know your value more than the ONE who assigned it to you?"

Today's Scripture:

Proverbs 14:30 (AMP) – *A calm and undisturbed mind and heart are the life and health of the body, but envy, jealousy, and wrath are like rottenness of the bones.*

Day 25 - A Fresh Start

"A fresh start is yours by My grace. For it is written, "My mercies are new every morning." Receive them and don't look back at your past. Let no one else define you. Let no other voice identify you. For I the Lord am your good Shepherd, raising you up for such a time as this. I the Lord am where your value and affirmation come from. You are in Me and I am in you, therefore you are empowered to be the person I have ordained you to be. You are strong in humility, loved in intimacy, and free in surrender."

Today's Scriptures:

Lamentations 3:22-23 – Through the Lord's mercies we are not consumed, because His compassions fail not. [23] They are new every morning; great is Your faithfulness.

John 14:20 – "In that day you will know that I am in My Father, and you are in Me, and I am in you."

Day 26 - Permanent Love

"I speak peace to you. Lock eyes with the One who has chosen you. Lock eyes with the One who has called and gifted you. Yes there are winds and there are waves, but both still know My Name. Both are still subject to Me. For I assure you that neither height nor depth, nor principality nor power, nor things past, present, or things to come can ever separate you from the love I have for you. My love for you is protecting, passionate, persevering, and yes, permanent. My love is full of vision and life. My love never fails."

Today's Scriptures:

Romans 8:38-39 – _For I am persuaded that neither death nor life, nor angels nor principalities nor powers, nor things present nor things to come, [39] nor height nor depth, nor any other created thing, shall be able to separate us from the love of God which is in Christ Jesus our Lord._

Day 27 - God's Protection

"Look to Me and be radiant. Do not fear for I am with you. It is written --no weapon formed against you shall prosper. I am your Shield and your Fortress. There is no need to self-protect, for I am who defends you and keeps you and not you yourself. There is warfare, but I am greater. There is conflict, but you are safe in Me. Fear not! Because you have loved Me; therefore, I will deliver you, I will set you securely on high for you have known My Name."

Today's Scriptures:

Psalm 91:14-16 – *"Because he has set his love upon Me, therefore I will deliver him; I will set him on high, because he has known My name. [15] He shall call upon Me, and I will answer him; I will be with him in trouble; I will deliver him and honor him. [16] With long life I will satisfy him, And show him My salvation."*

Day 28 - Cast Your Cares

"Be free My child as I encircle you with My Presence. Cast all your care on Me for I care for you. Have I not carried you this far? Have I not carried you through fire before? Worry has nothing for you. It doesn't add anything to you. In fact, it does much more taking than giving. I made your heart for peace, rest, and trust; not for anxiety. Remember, I have not given you a spirit of fear but power, love, and soundness of mind. Therefore, be confident, unshakeable, and invincible in My perfect love for you."

Today's Scriptures:

2 Timothy 1:7-9 – For God has not given us a spirit of fear, but of power and of love and of a sound mind. [8] Therefore do not be ashamed of the testimony of our Lord, nor of me His prisoner, but share with me in the sufferings for the gospel according to the power of God, [9] who has saved us and called us with a holy calling, not according to our works, but according to His own purpose and grace.

Day 29 - See What God Sees

"To the Spirit we go, for that's where life is derived, not the flesh. The Spirit gives life, love, and liberty, yet the flesh profits nothing. One contains My view and opinion and thus great grace and hope; the other contains all the limitations of the natural world. Let Me wash your eyes this day, let Me allow you to see what I see. For today I wash you in MY faith and MY belief. In Me and My perspective you are heightened, encouraged, and comforted. You are at home in My Spirit and My peace."

Today's Scriptures:

Romans 8:5-6 – For those who live according to the flesh set their minds on the things of the flesh, but those who live according to the Spirit, the things of the Spirit. ⁶ For to be carnally minded is death, but to be spiritually minded is life and peace.

2 Corinthians 3:17 – Now the Lord is the Spirit and where the Spirit of the Lord is there is liberty.

Day 30 - Arise To Victory

"Go ahead and arise. It's ok to get up again. I feel what you feel, I hurt when you hurt. Death couldn't keep Me down and disappointment is not going to keep you down. I know about temptation. I know about wounds. But I am no victim and neither are you. Do not fear, for Righteousness will always prevail. It is written into you. It is written into life itself. From My Spirit within, I will cause you to live out your destiny. I did not just die because of your sin, I also died to show you how much you matter to your Father in Heaven and to show you that you have value and purpose. Arise and live!"

Today's Scriptures:

Psalm 27:3 - Though an army may encamp against me, My heart shall not fear; Though war should rise against me, In this I will be confident.

1 John 5:4 – This is the victory that has overcome the world, even our faith.

Day 31 - God's Best You

"Come unto Me. I alone can heal your wounded heart. I alone can put the pieces together again. I alone can make you whole and complete. Unbound, unbroken, unwavering, and undeterred. Place your hand in Mine. Feel the warmth of My eternal touch as I cause your heart to dance and sing again and set you upon the path of your destiny. Others may delay it, but they will not defeat it. You are no imitation. You are an original. You're the best you I have and My Spirit looks good in you. Look at Me child. Look at Me and know you're safe and whole."

Today's Scriptures:

Psalm 107:20 – He sent His word and healed them, and delivered them from their destructions.

Isaiah 42:3 – A bruised reed He will not break, a smoking flax He will not quench; He will bring forth justice for truth.

Day 32 - Totally Clean

"Shine forth and celebrate the newness of My mercies every morning. Yesterday is past and today is a brand new opportunity to walk in My Spirit. I am not holding you back because of your past. What missteps have I ever held over your head? I do not hold your forgiveness hostage until you work hard enough for it. It is yours through the blood of My Son. My Spirit abiding inside you is proof I took care of your sin and proof of how clean I have made you!"

Today's Scriptures:

Lamentations 3:22-23 – _Through the LORD's mercies we are not consumed, because His compassions fail not. ²³ They are new every morning; great is Your faithfulness._

Hebrews 10:14 – _For by one offering Christ has perfected forever those who are being sanctified._

Day 33 - The Loyal One

"Rest. Peace. Still your heart before Me. You are clean because of the Word I have spoken over you: Valiant. Warrior. Chosen. Beloved. Adored. Mine. Yes, you are Mine. I am incapable of leaving or forsaking you. You have known rejection in your past but NOT from Me. I am the loyal One. Faithful and true. I began this good work in you and I WILL see it through. I am committed to you and your growth, development, and maturity. Hear My song and hear My voice as I heal, restore, and guide you into all truth."

Today's Scriptures:

John 16:13 – _"However, when He, the Spirit of Truth has come, He will guide you into all truth."_

John 15:3 – _"You are already clean because of the word which I have spoken over you."_

Day 34 - God's Workmanship

"Find rest. I am here. Do you not know that I am yours and you are Mine? Yes, you make your plans, but I order your steps. I am leading, guiding, and directing you in the paths of righteousness for My Name's sake. You must not forget who you are amidst life's ups and downs. You are chosen, bought with My own blood, appointed, anointed, My beloved, My workmanship -- created to bring light and life to this world. You are worth more than you have believed. Rest and relax in Me. Simply hold on to My unchanging hand, and when you cannot, know that I will still have hold of yours."

Today's Scriptures:

Psalm 23:3 – _He restores my soul; He leads me in the paths of righteousness for His name's sake._

John 15:16 (NIV) – _"You did not choose me, but I chose you and appointed you so that you might go and bear fruit--fruit that will last."_

Day 35 - Made For God

"Awaken unto Me, for I am abundant life and radiant health. My instructions are not burdensome but light—not weights but wings; for you are made for My ways, My attitudes, and My nature. You are made for love. Made for good will. Made for care and compassion. You are not self-centered, you are Christ-centered and others minded. Flee any and all ill will, grudges, and resentments. There is little that wreaks more havoc on your physical and emotional health than those. Your enemy tells you if you withhold love from others who hurt you it gives you power over them, but it is really how he tries to hold power over you."

Today's Scriptures:

Proverbs 17:22 (AMP) – A happy heart is good medicine and a cheerful mind works healing, but a broken spirit dries up the bones.

Romans 5:8 (NIV) – God demonstrates his own love for us in this: While we were still sinners Christ died for us.

Day 36 - Your Father's Love

"It's ok to let your heart sing again. Jesus loves me this I know -- this is no fairy tale song; it is foundational. My steadfast love keeps your heart anchored in even the most troubled waters. Know My love for you; believe it; never judge yourself unworthy of it! I don't love you because of what you do, I love you because of who I am. I don't love you because of the purity of your heart, I love you because of the purity of Mine. Know My love each day -- abide in it, feed on it. For My love is food indeed and fuel for living."

Today's Scriptures:

Titus 1:15 – To the pure all things are pure, but to those who are defiled and unbelieving nothing is pure.

1 John 4:16 – And we have known and believed the love God has for us. God is love, and He who abides in love abides in God, and God in Him.

Day 37 - The Central Miracle

"Be glad and winsome this day. Open up your heart and receive My divine entering of your spirit. All the miracles – the opening of blind eyes, the unstopping of deaf ears, the raising of the dead; all pale in comparison to My coming and living redemptively inside you! The new birth is the greatest miracle you or any other human can experience. That which is born of flesh is flesh but that which is born of My Spirit is of Me, eternally of Me. Knowing Me is not just written in Scripture, it is written into your very being."

Today's Scriptures:

John 3:4-6 – Nicodemus said to Him, "How can a man be born when he is old? Can he enter a second time into his mother's womb and be born?" 5 Jesus answered, "Truly, I say to you, unless one is born of water and the Spirit, he cannot enter the kingdom of God. 6 That which is born of the flesh is flesh, and that which is born of the Spirit is spirit."

Day 38 - Sons Not Slaves

"Oh that I came to you quietly and meekly in a manger. Do you perceive My true nature? I did not come imposing My rule with thunder and lightning raising My voice, "Obey or else!" That would not have created sons but slaves driven by fear. No, I have come humbly that I might cast out all fear and have many sons and daughters who know Me intimately. I have revealed the true nature of My Kingdom in My Son – who in truth is a King but He rules by and through a love-pierced heart rather than with force and fear. He is My divine 'yes' to you."

Today's Scriptures:

Luke 15:21-22 – And the son said, 'Father, I have sinned against heaven and in your sight, I am no longer worthy to be called your son.' 22 But the father said to his servants, 'Bring out the best robe and put it on him, and put a ring on his hand and sandals on his feet.'

Day 39 - Stay The Course

"Eyes on the prize My child. Eyes on the prize of the upward call I have given you. It is such a high calling and blessed assignment. Seek first My Kingdom and My righteousness and all else will be added to you. The 'all else' is not central nor can it be. It is My Kingdom and My righteousness that must be central and own the loyalty of your heart. There is freedom inside the fences I have given you. Trust Me. Hold to Me and My way. Stay the course. Disciplined. There is only bondage outside the boundaries I've set for you. Keep your eye single and your whole body will remain full of light."

Today's Scriptures:

Matthew 6:22 – *"The lamp of the body is the eye. If therefore your eye is good, your whole body will be full of light."*

Matthew 6:33 – *"But seek first the Kingdom of God and His righteousness, and all these things shall be added to you."*

Day 40 - Your Rock

"Arise beloved. For behold I declare you this day My invincible overcomer. More than a conqueror. In the natural world you will have trial and tribulation, but be of good cheer for I have overcome the natural world for you. I have become the door to the dimension of the Spirit where your peace of mind comes from. You are no longer subject, no longer easily overtaken, for I am the unshakeable foundation through which everything is built in your life. I am your stability, your anchor, your shelter; I am the immovable, unchanging One-- abide in and rely on Me."

Today's Scripture:

John 16:33 (AMP) – *"I have told you these things, so that in Me you may have perfect peace. In the world you will have tribulation, trial, distress, and frustration; but be of good cheer (be confident) for I have overcome the world (I have deprived it of its power to harm you and have conquered it for you.)"*

Day 41 - Your Freedom

"Take My hand and walk with Me. This is the day I have made, let us rejoice and be glad in it. Awaken unto righteousness and awaken unto your freedom. If the Son sets you free, you are free indeed. Not waiting to be free. Not trying to be free. FREE. Free to be all I say you are. Free to live out your true identity. Free to be clean, close, and intimate with Me each day. Free to no longer be mastered by sin or circumstances, not even the misguided intentions of others. FREE."

Today's Scriptures:

John 8:36 – "Therefore if the Son makes you free, you shall be free indeed."

1 Corinthians 15:34 – Awaken unto righteousness, and do not sin; for some do not have the knowledge of God.

Psalm 30:5 (TLB) – Weeping may go on for a night, but there is joy in the morning.

Day 42 - Taste And See

"Rest and receive of Me. Breathe Me in. Taste and see that I am good. Rejoice that My Presence is not to be earned, but is to be enjoyed. I am your Refuge and Fortress. Your ever present help in time of need. I am your Song and Strength, your Sun and Shield. Whatever you have need of -- I am. You need love? I am your love. You need peace? I am your peace. You need forgiveness? I am your forgiveness both when you receive it and when you give it. I am all these to you and through you, not because you're so good but because I'm so good."

Today's Scriptures:

Psalm 34:8 – *Oh, taste and see that the Lord is good; blessed is the man who trusts in Him!*

Psalm 91:2 – *I will say of the Lord, "He is my refuge and my fortress; my God, in Him I will trust."*

Day 43 - Your Identity

"Awaken unto your true identity. Understand who I say you are. You are not an unrighteous being trying to "be righteous." I am not asking you to be something you're not, I'm admonishing you to be who I've put in you to be. Your enemy wants to deal with your behavior, I want to deal with your beliefs about how you see yourself. For as a man thinks in his heart so is he. Therefore, be careful what self-views and definitions you allow into your heart and mind. Be careful who and what you let define you. Do they line up with Me? Do they line up with My words about you? If you will but see you are a joint heir in My Kingdom, tremendous empowerment awaits."

Today's Scriptures:

Romans 8:14 – *For as many as are led by the Spirit of God, these are sons of God.*

Proverbs 23:7 – *For as he thinks in his heart, so is he.*

Day 44 - A Divine Exchange

"Come forth My love. You are no longer bound but you are free indeed. And your freedom did not begin with your behavior but with Mine. For My cross has allowed you to reap what I sowed. It has allowed you to drink the fruit of My vine rather than yours. A divine exchange has occurred. Your unrighteousness for My righteousness. Your resentments for My forgiveness. I have made you clean and holy, not you yourself. Walk in the joy of My freedom as you start your day not with behavior, but with believing the truth of all I have done for you."

Today's Scriptures:

1 Corinthians 1:18 – For the message of the cross is foolishness to those who are perishing, but to us who are being saved it is the power of God.

John 6:27 (NLT) – Jesus told them, "This is the only work God wants from you: Believe in the One He has sent."

Day 45 - Your Protection

"Beloved, set your heart. Set your mind. Allow Me to anchor your soul, for I am your Refuge and Fortress. Despite what goes on around you, you have peace. For peace is not the absence of difficulty, it's the presence of someone greater than the difficulty. It's not the absence of fire, it's the presence of someone with greater authority than the fire. I did not put out the flame inside Nebuchadnezzar's furnace, I demonstrated My authority over it. Were they not unharmed and unburned because of My Presence? Trust in Me, I am the greater One and I am present in you."

Today's Scriptures:

1 Corinthians 3:16 – _Do you not know that you are the temple of God and that the Spirit of God dwells in you?_

John 14:27 – _"Peace I leave with you, My peace I give to you; not as the world gives do I give to you. Let not your heart be troubled, neither let it be afraid."_

Day 46 - God's Masterpiece

"Stand. You are a brand new creation. By its mere definition, you are not who you used to be! Do not let the enemy tell you otherwise. Do not let him lock you into old identities. You are My own handiwork, My masterpiece, created new in Christ Jesus for good works. The truest realities about you are the things I say about you. Elevate My truth over your feelings, over the opinions of others, over your behavior, and even over your thoughts about yourself. Humility isn't that you never say anything good about yourself; humility simply agrees with the value assigned to you by your Creator."

Today's Scriptures:

1 Corinthians 6:11 – *And such were some of you. But you were washed, you were sanctified, you were justified in the Name of the Lord Jesus and by the Spirit of our God.*

Ephesians 2:10 – *For we are His workmanship, created in Christ for good works, which God prepared before that we should walk in them.*

Day 47 - Living Full

"Revel in fullness of joy as you see the fruits of feeding on Me. Let us continue in this season. No longer will you be ruled by things that are no reflection of who you are. What have your circumstances or the opinions of others ever had to do with your value and true identity? No longer are you in survival mode, always in desperate need of love; needing every circumstance to go your way; but you are becoming an expression of My love day in and day out. You are living full and complete in Me, lacking nothing."

Today's Scriptures:

Psalm 23:1 – The Lord is my Shepherd I shall not want.

Colossians 2:10 (NLT) – So you also are complete through your union with Christ, who is the head over every ruler and authority.

John 15:9 (NIV) – "As the Father has loved Me, so have I loved you."

Day 48 - Inwardly Sourced

"I am your Source, so treat others how I have treated you. Love others how I have loved you. Why put your character and happiness in someone else's hands? I am your Vine-- not them. Be generous toward others as I have been generous toward you. For it is written, "The wrath of man does not work the righteousness of God". In other words, your attempts at controlling people or circumstances with anger do much more harm than good. So forgive, even as I have already forgiven you. Be at peace with all men even as I am already at peace with you."

Today's Scriptures:

James 1:20 – For the wrath of man does not produce the righteousness of God.

Luke 6:31 – "Do unto others as you would have them do unto you."

Romans 12:18 – If it is possible, as much as it depends on you, live peaceably with all men.

Day 49 - Dance Again

"Do not fret, do not fear. For I will rebuild you. I will renew you from the inside out. I will remake you, restore you once again. No longer shall the enemy hold sway over you for I am your Deliverer and your Defender. I say to you, "You WILL dance again with laughter. You WILL sing again with joy." For I am the Lord who heals you. Nothing is too difficult for Me. Behold, by My Spirit, I turn your grief into gladness and your pain into purpose. Receive of Me. Drink of Me. Take My words within you as you would take in medicine. For it is written, "My words are Spirit and they are life - health to your flesh and healing to your bones."

Today's Scriptures:

Romans 8:5 – For those who live according to the flesh set their minds on the things of the flesh, but those who live according to the Spirit, the things of the Spirit.

Psalm 30:2 – O Lord My God, I cried out to You, and You have healed me.

Day 50 - Why He Came

"Open up your heart to My comfort. Open up your mind to My renewing. You see your mistakes, your missteps, and the resulting shame - but I see the reason I came. I cannot quit on you, I came for you. I came to heal you. I came to rescue you. I came to reveal to you who you really are. I didn't just die to save you, I died to show you how much you mean to the Father. I came to show you your real value. Don't ever let the enemy convince you that you are a disappointment to Me. I've always known your potential, destiny, identity, and eternal purpose; that's why I came."

Today's Scriptures:

Isaiah 43:1 – But now, thus says the Lord, who created you, O Jacob, And He who formed you, O Israel: "Fear not, for I have redeemed you; I have called you by your name; You are Mine."

Psalm 147:3 (NIV) – He heals the broken hearted and binds up their wounds.

Day 51 - Made For Him

"Every cell of your being is made by Me and for Me. The living Spirit of Christ in you is the right way to think, act, feel, and be in every conceivable situation. My Son, whom I have given to you and to the entire world, revealed that everything in creation is made to work His way. I predestined you to be conformed to His image so much so that your very heart and body sing when His light and life shine through you. This is My love for you. This is truth and reality, not random philosophy."

Today's Scriptures:

Colossians 1:15-17 (NLT) – Christ is the image of the invisible God. The firstborn over all creation. [16] For by Him all things were created that are in heaven and that are on earth, visible and invisible, whether thrones or dominions or principalities or powers. All things were created through Him and for Him. [17] And He is before all things, and in Him all things consist.

Day 52 - God's Plans

"Be still and listen for MY voice. For one of the deceptions of your enemy is to tell you I want nothing to do with you - when in truth I am the One who justified you, redeemed you, chose you, and reconciled you to Myself. Your recent struggles are not over your past, they are over your future. For I have so much ahead of you, so many great plans for you. The enemy is trying to knock you off your destiny, but I am your joy and your strength! For I have overcome him for you, and I overcome him through you."

Today's Scriptures:

Revelation 12:11 – And they overcame him by the blood of the Lamb and by the word of their testimony, and they did not love their lives to the death.

Romans 8:31 – What then shall we say to these things? If God is for us, who can be against us?

Day 53 - Your True Self

"Come away with Me - into the quiet, into the secret place. For it is here that I strip away your false self and show you your true self. You are not the sum total of your mistakes, you are the sum total of who I've made you to be in your spirit man. I do not ask you to earn your way with Me, I only ask that you actively participate with everything I already say that you are. Come to know Me, for once you know who I am, you're on your way to knowing who you are."

Today's Scriptures:

Psalm 91:1-2 – He who dwells in the secret place of the Most High shall abide under the shadow of the Almighty. 2 I will say of the Lord, "He is my refuge and my fortress; My God, in Him I will trust."

Matthew 16:16 – Simon Peter answered, "You are the Christ, the Son of the living God."

Day 54 - His Is Yours

"Stop, listen, and see. What a difference there is between your trying to get yourself reconciled to Me and actively participating with the reconciliation I have given you. Your way is difficult and heavy; My way is freeing and empowering. Because I am in you, do you not reap what I sowed? I tell you truly, yes. What is Mine is yours. My victory, your victory; My love, your love; My righteousness, your righteousness; My purity, your purity. Enter in, participate with Me and all I have done."

Today's Scriptures:

John 16:14 – *"He will glorify Me, for He will take of what is Mine and declare it to you."*

Romans 8:16-17 – *The Spirit Himself bears witness with our spirit that we are children of God, [17] and if children, then heirs – heirs of God and joint heirs with Christ.*

Day 55 - Living Full

"In quietness and trust is your strength. Take of Me. As freely as you have received, freely give. I supply you joy, you release it to those around you. I supply you forgiveness, you extend it to those around you. Every day you have the opportunity to live supernaturally with Me as your source-- not the world. When others harm you, forgive them – allowing Me to supply to you the love and substance they did not. That way you never leave trouble makers empty-handed, but full once again."

Today's Scriptures:

Hebrews 13:5 (AMP) – _For God has said, "I_ WILL NEVER _[under any circumstances]_ DESERT YOU _[nor give you up nor leave you without support, nor will I in any degree leave you helpless],_ NOR WILL I FORSAKE _or_ LET YOU DOWN _or relax My hold on you!"_

Matthew 10:8 – _"Heal the sick, raise the dead, cleanse those who have leprosy, drive out demons. Freely you have received; freely give."_

Day 56 - Your Healing

"My heart longs for you. I look upon you with great compassion. Do you not know that whatever falls on you falls on Me? Where you hurt I hurt, where you suffer I suffer. I am touched with the very feelings of your infirmities and humanity. I am with you, I am in you, I am committed to you always even until the end of the age. Yield your pain and disappointments to Me. For I am the rebuilder of that which is broken. I am your healing."

Today's Scriptures:

Hebrews 4:15 (NIV) – For we do not have a high priest who is unable to empathize with our weaknesses, but we have one who has been tempted in every way, just as we are--yet He did not sin.

Jeremiah 17:14 – Heal me, O Lord, and I shall be healed; Save me, and I shall be saved, for You are My praise.

Day 57 - Loving Others

"Let My cup refresh you. Let My river run through you. Let My radiance extend far beyond you. For am I not interested in the lost and broken? I tell you truly I am. My heart breaks for humanity and the lost-ness man has chosen in ignorance. Let us reach out to them together. You in Me and I in you; not just sharing the way but showing the way. Be too glad, too good, and too great a person to be the enemy of any man."

Today's Scriptures:

2 Corinthians 5:18-20 – Now all things are of God, who has reconciled us to Himself through Jesus Christ, and has given us the ministry of reconciliation, [19] that is, that God was in Christ reconciling the world to Himself, not imputing their trespasses to them, and has committed to us the word of reconciliation. [20] Now then, we are ambassadors for Christ, as though God were pleading through us: we implore you on Christ's behalf, be reconciled to God.

Day 58 - Do Not Worry

"In the quietness of your heart, I am here. Yes, I am very aware of the decisions that are ahead of you, but I am not worried and neither should you be. Just walk with Me, daily seek Me first, and I will get you where you need to be. Do not yield to rapid fire thoughts and speculations; they are laced with fear from your enemy. You live, you love, you abide in Me. Do not pray for deliverance, I will grace and empower you to overcome by My Spirit. Do not strive to be good; but instead surrender to My goodness that is within you. Behold, I am with you always. Behold, I will carry you through."

Today's Scriptures:

2 Corinthians 10:5 – Casting down arguments and every high thing that exalts itself against the knowledge of God, bringing every thought into captivity to the obedience of Christ.

Matthew 6:34 – "Therefore do not worry about tomorrow, for tomorrow will worry about its own things."

Day 59 - Release Your Pain

"Release it all to Me. Your hurt, your pain, your disappointment. They were never yours to carry. If you allow Me, I will take them from you and give you beauty for ashes, joy for mourning, and fresh water for bitter. Yes, I do see those things. Yes, I do see what you try to hide. Yes, I see your brokenness and yes, I love you anyway. You are made for Me. Fearfully and wonderfully made for Me. Letting Me in is as natural as letting air into your lungs. You do not fix yourself then come to Me; instead, come as you are."

Today's Scriptures:

Psalm 55:22 (TLB) – *Give your burdens to the Lord. He will carry them. He will not permit the Godly to slip or fall.*

Psalm 68:19 (NIV) – *Praise be to the Lord, to God our Savior, who daily bears our burdens.*

Day 60 - Eternally His

"You belong to Me; and because you belong to Me, you should no longer look down on yourself. You are forever accepted as My beloved. Why would you hate what I love? Why would you reject what I accept? Why would you call unclean what I have personally made clean? Instead, let all that you are and all that you do be colored with humble gratitude for what I have done for you, with you, and in you. You are eternally Mine, let your heart rejoice."

Today's Scriptures:

Acts 10:15 – *What God has cleansed you must not call common.*

Ephesians 1:4-6 – *He chose us in Him before the foundation of the world, that we should be holy and without blame before Him in love, 5 having predestined us as adopted by Christ to Himself, according to the pleasure of His will, 6 to the praise of the glory of His grace, by which He made us accepted in the Beloved.*

Day 61 - Your Supply

"I am your Supply. Do not put your happiness in the hands of others but instead look to Me. For you are made for Me. Only I can deeply satisfy you. More important than your love for Me is My love for you. So receive it, actively participate with it. It is yours, not to earn, but to share. For what did you not get when I gave you the gift of Myself? What did you not get when My love was shed abroad in your heart? My Spirit gives life. My Spirit is life. Walk by it, talk by it, live by it, speak by it."

Today's Scriptures:

Romans 5:5 – Now hope does not disappoint, because the love of God has been poured out in our hearts by the Holy Spirit who was given to us.

Galatians 4:6 – And because you are sons, God has sent forth the Spirit of His Son into your hearts, crying out, "Abba, Father!"

Day 62 - True Intimacy

"Look to Me. Lean into Me. Yes, works are good but intimacy is better. The law is good but love is better. Sacrifice is good but mercy is better. Do not live FOR Me in your own efforts, but live FROM Me as your Source. For more than I desire outward conformity, I desire inward transformation; and giving you a new heart, My heart. No act of ritual, however devout, can ever take the place of true intimacy with Me and genuine love for your fellow man."

Today's Scriptures:

Ezekiel 36:26 (NIV) – *"I will give you a new heart and put a new spirit in you; I will remove from you your heart of stone and give you a heart of flesh."*

Galatians 4:19 (NLT) – *Oh, my dear children! I feel as if I'm going through labor pains for you again, and they will continue until Christ is fully developed in your lives.*

Day 63 - Do Not Hide

"As light is to the eye, as beauty is to nature, as oxygen is to lungs; so are you and I affinities. We belong together. Do not listen to the enemy tell you to hide from Me. He's just trying to keep you from the very help you need. Why would you judge yourself unworthy of My love when I am the One who made you worthy to receive it? You cannot earn your way with Me; you simply recognize your need of Me then open up your heart to receive. In this New Covenant, I am the Initiator; you are the responder. Your role is not to make yourself worthy enough to receive something, it is to participate with all I have provided you."

Today's Scriptures:

John 14:1 (NIV) – *"Do not let your hearts be troubled. Trust in God; trust also in Me."*

Hebrews 9:12 – *With His own blood Christ entered the Most Holy Place once for all, having obtained for us an eternal redemption.*

Day 64 - The Word of God

"Why be so hung up on the words of others when one word from Me can change everything? My words have creative, healing, and life-giving power that cover you in strength, righteousness, and glory. My words stop the mouth of the accuser; they stay the hand of the adversary. They lift your head in times of doubt and distress. They heal and they restore. Only believe My child, and enjoy the real reality."

Today's Scriptures:

Psalm 119:9 – *How can a young man cleanse his way? By taking heed according to Your word.*

Psalm 119:105 – *Your word is a lamp to my feet And a light to my path.*

Isaiah 40:8 – *The grass withers, the flower fades, But the word of our God stands forever.*

Day 65 - Your Purpose

"I can't have you down. I can't have you locked into discouragement. For you are My light and My salt in this world. My purpose summoned your very existence. Would I have made you had you not been carrying something your generation has need of? I tell you truly you are fearfully and wonderfully made. You are NOT random. You are NOT by chance. You are here on purpose for a purpose and you are MINE."

Today's Scriptures:

Psalm 43:5 – Why are you cast down, O my soul? And why are you disquieted within me? Hope in God; For I shall yet praise Him, the help of my countenance and my God.

Psalm 73:26 – My flesh and my heart fail; But God is the strength of my heart and my portion forever.

Psalm 40:2 – He also brought me up out of a horrible pit, Out of the miry clay, and set my feet upon a rock, and established my steps.

Day 66 - Marked By God

"Arise and go forth. For I have given you My Name, My Word, My Spirit, My blood, My Life, My Kingdom, and My authority. No longer do you carry the mark of past sins, you carry the mark of My Presence. For through you I release the fragrance of My reality everywhere you go. You did not reap what you sowed, you reaped what I sowed. Therefore, you carry life for death, peace for unrest, love for hate, and joy for mourning."

Today's Scriptures:

Romans 14:17 (NIV) – For the Kingdom of God is not a matter of eating and drinking, but of righteousness, peace, and joy in the Holy Spirit.

Matthew 28:18-19 – And Jesus came and spoke to them, saying, "All authority has been given to Me in heaven and on earth. [19] Go therefore and make disciples of all the nations, baptizing them in the name of the Father and of the Son and of the Holy Spirit."

Day 67 - Your Supply

"Rest. Rely. Receive. Why do you live as though it's all up to you? Why do you live as though you have to make it all happen? I tell you the truth, My grace is sufficient for you. I am the Supplier and you are the receiver. You love because I first loved you. You forgive because I first forgave you. You are kind because I am kind to you. Do not live trying to earn from Me; instead live from all that you have already received from Me."

Today's Scriptures:

1 Corinthians 15:10 – But by the grace of God I am what I am, and His grace toward me was not in vain; but I labored more abundantly than they all, yet not I, but the grace of God which was with me.

Romans 12:6 – Having then gifts differing according to the grace that is given to us, let us use them: if prophecy, let us prophesy in proportion to our faith.

Day 68 - Living Healthy

"Be blessed My child. Yield your mind and any wayward thoughts to Me. For My pleasant words and thoughts are sweet to your soul and healing to your body. The more healthy your thoughts, the more healthy the rest of you is. Let Me cleanse you of all your fears, worries, and any resentments. For harboring resentments is like harboring a poison. Do not try to enslave others through a grudge for that only enslaves you."

Today's Scriptures:

Psalm 85:8 – I will hear what God the Lord will speak, for He will speak peace to His people and to His saints.

Colossians 3:12-13 – Therefore, as the elect of God, holy and beloved, put on tender mercies, kindness, humility, meekness, longsuffering; [13] bearing with one another, and forgiving one another, if anyone has a complaint against another; even as Christ forgave you, so you also must do.

Day 69 - An Easy Yoke

"Take of Me. I am not your demand, I am your Supply. My yoke is not heavy on you, My yoke is easy. Flee the burdensome religious deception that invites you to try to become something you already are and to work for things you already have. What have I not already accomplished for you? You are blessed; not trying to become blessed. You are loved; not trying to become loved. You are justified; not trying to become justified. Do not work for these; thank Me for these."

Today's Scriptures:

Matthew 11:28 – *"Come to me, all you who are weary and burdened, and I will give you rest."*

Zephaniah 3:17 – *For the LORD your God is living among you. He is a mighty savior. He will take delight in you with gladness. With His love, He will calm all your fears. He will rejoice over you with joyful songs.*

Day 70 - Rest In Him

"Slow down. Don't be in such a hurry. Please do not hide from Me behind all your activity. Until you learn to rest and pause in Me, you will never fully understand and appreciate all I have done for you. I am training you in quietness and rest so your life, strength, and plans each day come from Me, not from the pressures of this world. Walk with Me, talk with Me; I will help you see the pain behind the pain and the hurt behind the hurt that you so long to understand."

Today's Scriptures:

Psalm 46:10 – Be still and know that I am God.

1 John 4:9-10 (NLT) – God showed how much He loved us by sending His one and only Son into the world so that we might have eternal life through Him. [10] This is real love—not that we loved God, but that He loved us and sent His Son as a sacrifice to take away our sins.

Day 71 - Free Indeed

"Freedom. Glorious freedom. It is what I made you for. It was for freedom I set you free. It is true -- He who the Son sets free is free indeed. You are free, no more shackles, no more chains. Love has won! Even if you misstep, you are free. Even if you feel off, you are free. Even your behavior doesn't determine whether you are free, it simply reveals whether you agree with the reality of your freedom in Me. For you don't cause your freedom, you discover it then identify with it!"

Today's Scriptures:

John 8:36 – *"If therefore the Son makes you free, you shall be free indeed."*

Galatians 5:1 – *Stand fast therefore in the liberty by which Christ has made us free, and do not be entangled again with a yoke of bondage.*

Day 72 - The Holy Spirit

"When you embrace My Spirit, you embrace Me. The Holy Spirit is your birthright as My child. He belongs to you and you belong to Him. He is the guaranty of your inheritance. As you find a deeper surrender of yourself you will find a deeper fullness of the Holy Spirit. He is My natural and normal Presence inside you. He convicts you, converts you, commissions you, and conforms you to My likeness. He guides you into all truth and is your Teacher, Comforter, and Friend. Don't resist Him, receive Him and let Him lead."

Today's Scriptures:

John 14:16-18 – *"And I will pray the Father, and He will give you another Helper, that He may abide with you forever—[17] the Spirit of truth, whom the world cannot receive, because it neither sees Him nor knows Him; but you know Him, for He dwells with you and will be in you. [18] I will not leave you orphans; I will come to you."*

Day 73 - Rise Again

"The past is just that, the past. Don't be held back by it. Don't be constrained by it. Have I not promised to work all things for your good? Yes, even your failures become successes to Me. I am greater than any circumstance. My grace is greater. My love is greater. I tell you truly, you are fully known and still fully loved. You cannot fail; as I WILL complete in you what I have begun in you. Simply rise, rest, receive, and abide."

Today's Scriptures:

Philippians 1:6 – Being confident of this very thing, that He who has begun a good work in you will complete it until the day of Jesus Christ.

1 John 3:16 (NIV) – This is how we know what love is: Jesus Christ laid down his life for us. And we ought to lay down our lives for our brothers and sisters.

Day 74 - True Greatness

"Dare to be great, but not great as the world seeks after greatness. Great in surrender, great in humility, great in receptivity. Be great in depending on Me, great at letting the past go, great at forgiving others, great at serving your children, your family, and even those who hurt you. Dare to be great, but be great in all the things I supply you greatness in. Great in what matters far more than money or status."

Today's Scriptures:

Matthew 20:26 – "It shall not be so among you. But whoever would be great among you must be your servant."

John 13:3-5 – Jesus, knowing that the Father had given all things into His hands, and that He had come from God and was going to God, ⁴ rose from supper and laid aside His garments, took a towel and girded Himself. ⁵ After that, He poured water into a basin and began to wash the disciples' feet, and to wipe them with the towel with which He was girded.

Day 75 - A Victorious Life

"Take My hand, knowing nothing is too difficult for Me. For no matter what you face, I ALWAYS lead you in triumph and THROUGH you release the revelation of My character to others. What many see as obstacles, you and I see as opportunities. Opportunities to reveal the victory of life in My Spirit and the invincibility of love from a pure heart. While others may try to be the source of your bad attitudes I shall be the Source of your good attitudes."

Today's Scriptures:

2 Corinthians 2:14 – _Now thanks be to God who always leads us in triumph in Christ, and through us diffuses the fragrance of His knowledge in every place._

1 John 5:4-5 – _For whatever is born of God overcomes the world. And this is the victory that has overcome the world--our faith._ [5] _Who is he who overcomes the world, but he who believes that Jesus is the Son of God?_

Day 76 - Be Confident

"Fear not for I am with you. Do not cast away your confidence as I show you once again who and whose you are. Do not bow the knee to the oppression of adversity nor give way to the thief of speculation. They want nothing more than to steal your joy which is your strength. Bind spirits of confusion, silence the voice of your accuser, rise and be everything I have made you to be. Do I not know your end from your beginning? Truly I do. For you are not the same person you once were; you are redeemed in Me."

Today's Scriptures:

Psalm 16:11 – You will show me the path of life; In Your presence is fullness of joy; At Your right hand are pleasures forevermore.

Hebrews 10:35 – Therefore do not cast away your confidence, which has great reward.

Day 77 - Inwardly Sourced

"Rest and receive as you abide in Me this day. As your good and faithful Husband, I lead you by what I supply; not by what I demand, so live freely from My eternal resources. Live bountifully out of overflow. For you are not deficient in love, you are sufficient in love. You are not deficient in gentleness, you are sufficient in gentleness. You are not deficient in self-control, you are sufficient in self-control. Nothing by achieving, all by receiving. I am everything you need, simply abide in Me."

Today's Scriptures:

Colossians 2:6-7 – As you therefore have received Christ Jesus the Lord, so walk in Him, [7] rooted and built up in Him and established in the faith.

Galatians 5:22-23 – But the fruit of the Spirit is love, joy, peace, longsuffering, kindness, goodness, faithfulness, [23] gentleness, self-control. Against such there is no law.

Day 78 - Complete In Christ

"Hear My voice. You are enough. Cease from your striving and straining. Cease your attempts to get from others what you need to get first from Me. You are adequate in Me. You are complete in Me. The moment you set out to hear you are "enough" in the opinions of others, you reveal you do not believe you're enough in Me. Yet they cannot give you the validation you seek, only I can. They cannot satisfy you, only I can. Hear My voice. You are enough."

Today's Scriptures:

Psalm 23:1-2 (NLT) – The LORD is my Shepherd; I have all that I need. ² He lets me rest in green meadows; He leads me beside peaceful streams.

Colossians 2:9-10 (GWT) – All of God lives in Christ's body, ¹⁰ and God has made you complete in Christ. Christ is in charge of every ruler and authority.

Day 79 - God's Plan

Hear My heart My child. Hear My strong yet tender heart beat for you. For before there was time I knew you and had you in mind. Then came your creation; such wonderful things I have woven into your tapestry. Then came your manifestation as My very own child - born of My Spirit, washed anew in My blood. Now is your transformation - as I conform you and grow you into My very own image and likeness. Completing what I always had in mind for you. For I delight in shaping you toward the only image you were ever created to bear - Mine."

Today's Scriptures:

Matthew 22:20-21 – And Jesus said to them, "Whose image and inscription is this?" 21 They said to Him, "Caesar's." And He said to them, "Render therefore to Caesar the things that are Caesar's, and to God the things that are God's."

Day 80 - God's Perspective

"Look at Me and live. Behold as in a mirror My glory. Be held by My glory, My perspective, and My opinion as your inner man yields. Do not get caught looking too much into natural things; your behavior, your actions, your own thoughts about yourself. Do not overvalue the natural and undervalue the Spirit where the truth is. Do not overvalue your mistakes, and undervalue My mercy. Do not overvalue your past, and undervalue My love. It's ok to believe all I've done for you, all I've made you, and all I've said about you, it was all My idea. Rest in Me, walk with Me, look at Me and live."

Today's Scripture:

2 Corinthians 3:18 (NLT) – *So all of us who have had that veil removed can see and reflect the glory of the Lord. And the Lord—who is the Spirit—makes us more and more like him as we are changed into his glorious image.*

Day 81 - God's Voice

"Be at peace, be at rest. Stay dependent, abiding, humble, listening from within. I am not the voice that condemns or rejects you, I am the Voice who justifies, encourages, and empowers you. Remember, you do not gain My love through self-control, you gain self-control through My love. As you rest, embrace Me. Flee the lies. Flee the false realities of this world. Sin is the parent of misery. You cannot make it the parent of happiness no matter how hard one may try. Come abide with Me in Spirit and in Truth."

Today's Scriptures:

John 8:10-11 – When Jesus had raised Himself up and saw no one but the woman, He said to her, "Woman, where are those accusers of yours? Has no one condemned you?" 11 She said, "No one, Lord." And Jesus said to her, "Neither do I condemn you; go and sin no more."

Day 82 - Flee Fear

"Come alive with joy and healing this day. For My glory has risen upon you. The world did not supply your joy, so the world cannot take it away. There is no safety within your walls of defense, only loneliness and isolation - just what the enemy wants. So rise with Me and I will protect you. I will be your rear guard, your fortress, your defense. Fling away your fears in exchange for freedom. Freedom in Me. The freedom you are made for."

Today's Scriptures:

Isaiah 41:13 (NIV) – *"For I am the LORD your God who takes hold of your right hand and says to you, Do not fear; I will help you."*

Isaiah 43:1 (NIV) – *But now, this is what the LORD says-- he who created you, Jacob, he who formed you, Israel: "Do not fear, for I have redeemed you; I have summoned you by name; you are mine."*

Day 83 - God's Faithfulness

"Fear not for I am with you. Even when you're unfaithful, I remain faithful. Good days or bad days do not sway Me. When you are down I am there. When you are up I am there. When you cry I am there. When you laugh I am there. In your valleys I am there. On your mountains I am there. My loyalty to you is not because of what you do but because of who I am. Hold to My unfailing love and unchanging character."

Today's Scriptures:

Luke 12:6-7 (NIV) – "Are not five sparrows sold for two cents? Yet not one of them is forgotten before God. [7] Indeed, the very hairs of your head are all numbered. Do not fear; you are more valuable than many sparrows."

2 Timothy 2:13 (NLT) – If we are unfaithful, He remains faithful, for He cannot deny who He is.

Hebrews 13:5 - For He Himself has said, "I will never leave you nor forsake you."

Day 84 - Deeper In Christ

"I want to take you deeper. Deeper into Me and deeper into who I am. Deeper into intimacy. Deeper into surrender. Deeper into freedom. I want to show you what it is to love the Lord your God with all your heart, mind, soul, and strength. To show you what it is to truly be My disciple. Will you surrender more of your heart to Me? Will you allow Me to immerse you fully in My love? You have all of Me; may I have all of you?"

Today's Scriptures:

1 John 3:1 (NIV) – *How great is the love the Father has lavished on us, that we should be called children of God!*

John 15:26 (TLB) – *"But I will send you the Comforter – the Holy Spirit, the source of all truth. He will come to you from the Father and will tell you all about Me."*

Day 85 - Fully Equipped

"Awaken unto Me. Hear My voice and do not cast away your confidence. You are fully equipped in Me. Live and know I am with you. Live and know your past is forgiven. Live and know with full assurance I have called you as a difference maker. You not only belong, you belong to Me. You not only are strong, you are strong in My strength. You not only are alive, you are alive in and by My Spirit. Keep the faith. Walk in Truth. Let Me defend you and not your own lips."

Today's Scriptures:

Joel 3:10 – *Let the weak say, "I am strong."*

Colossians 3:1-3 – *If then you were raised with Christ, seek those things which are above, where Christ is, sitting at the right hand of God. ² Set your mind on things above, not on things on the earth. ³ For you died, and your life is hidden with Christ in God.*

Day 86 - The Nature of God

"When there is no other, I am here. I am the I am. I am a friend that sticks closer than a brother. I am your ever present help in time of need. I am your River in the desert. I am your Peace in the midst of the storm. I am the master Light of all your seeing. I am your Constant, your Anchor, your Rock. When all other ground is shifting sand, I do not change. I am your Comforter and Friend, your Refuge in the day of trouble. I am your Everlasting Father. Do not turn from Me or My ways. For when you stay true to Me, you stay true to your highest good."

Today's Scriptures:

Hebrews 13:8 – Jesus Christ is the same yesterday and today and forever.

Colossians 1:15 (NLT) – Christ is the visible image of the invisible God. He existed before anything was created and is supreme over all creation.

Day 87 - Satisfied In Christ

"Rest and receive, My child. Always keep your heart open to My Word. Do not allow people and things to take your confidence from you-- they didn't give it to you so they can't take it away. Abide in Me as your daily Source and Supply. No one can satisfy you like I satisfy you. I have cornered the market on human fulfillment. Therefore, do not look to others to give you something that only I can provide. You set them up for failure, and you set yourself up for disappointment."

Today's Scriptures:

Colossians 1:16 – For by Him all things were created that are in heaven and that are on earth, visible and invisible, whether thrones or dominions or principalities or powers. All things were created through Him and for Him.

Mark 5:15 – Then they came to Jesus and saw the one who had been demon-possessed and had the legion, he was sitting and clothed and in his right mind.

Day 88 - Overcoming Your Past

"My forgiveness is received-- not deserved. Could you really ever do enough to merit your own forgiveness? No, but My Son has achieved forgiveness for you through His blood. Therefore, do not let the enemy lock you into your past, for his aim is to render you ineffective in your present. We have too much work to do in your family, too many people that need your help and guidance for you to spend all of your time trying to qualify yourself to be used. My Son has already qualified you. Let go of what's behind you so you can grab what's ahead of you."

Today's Scriptures:

Colossians 1:21-22 – *And you, who once were alienated and enemies in your mind by wicked works, yet now He has reconciled* [22] *in the body of His flesh through death, to present you holy, and blameless, and above reproach in His sight.*

Day 89 - Old Garments

"Throw off your old garment and follow Me. Do not let the enemy tell you that you have not changed! You have not only changed, you have been transformed by My grace, love, and power at work within you. I have made you new. Just because not every outer behavior you have lines up yet doesn't mean your transformation is not real or has not taken root. Trust in Me, abide in Me, and let's continue to walk together."

Today's Scriptures:

Mark 10:49-52 (NIV) – Jesus stopped and said, "Call him." So they called to the blind man, "Cheer up! On your feet! He's calling you." [50] Throwing his cloak aside, he jumped to his feet and came to Jesus. [51] "What do you want me to do for you?" Jesus asked him. The blind man said, "Rabbi, I want to see." [52] "Go," said Jesus, "your faith has healed you." Immediately he received his sight and followed Jesus along the road.

Day 90 - Christ's Companionship

"Hear Me call, My child. My heart beats for you. I long to draw you in. Into My peace, My comfort, My safety. There is refuge here in the shadow of My wings. So few take the time to find it, but you are different. You long for the sweet, satisfying companionship that belongs to those who revere and respect the Lord. You long for My perspective. I will spend eternity showing you My covenant and revealing its deep inner meaning."

Today's Scriptures:

Psalm 25:14 (AMP) – The secret [of the sweet, satisfying companionship] of the Lord have they who fear (revere and worship) Him, and He will show them His covenant and reveal to them its [deep, inner] meaning.

John 16:13 (GNT) – "When, however, the Spirit comes, who reveals the truth about God, He will lead you into all the truth."

Day 91 - Amazing Grace

"As praise and thanksgiving resonate through your mind, body, and spirit this day, allow My love to overtake you. Look what I have done for you. Look what I have done in you. Look what I have done through you! Amazing and again I say amazing grace. Love those I have given you with a servant's heart. Give expecting nothing in return. Stay humble, stay dependent, and I will show Myself strong. Today I continue through you in great power and might; lifting you to brand new heights."

Today's Scriptures:

1 Corinthians 15:10 – But by the grace of God I am what I am, and His grace toward me was not in vain; but I labored more abundantly than they all, yet not I, but the grace of God which was with me.

2 Chronicles 16:9 – For the eyes of the Lord run to and fro throughout the whole earth, to show Himself strong on behalf of those whose heart is loyal to Him.

Day 92 - Leadership

"Lead. Lead. Lead. Not the way the world does, but rather as I do -- by serving. Greatness to Me is not how many serve you but how many you serve. Do not let the opinions of others define you. Be strong where it matters, in love and truth. Be rich where it matters - in kindness and generosity and in the true riches of My Kingdom. Let My virtues do all your promoting. I am ever before you. I am your shield and rear guard. I am in you."

Today's Scriptures:

Matthew 20:25-28 – But Jesus called them to Himself and said, "You know that the rulers of the Gentiles lord it over them, and those who are great exercise authority over them. [26] Yet it shall not be so among you; but whoever desires to become great among you, let him be your servant. [27] And whoever desires to be first among you, let him be your slave—[28] just as the Son of Man did not come to be served, but to serve, and to give His life a ransom for many."

Day 93 - Flee Fear

"Be not afraid, only believe. Rather than try harder to trust Me, simply get to know Me better. For as you know Me, you will trust Me - you will see and trust My character, see and trust My heart, see and trust My guiding hand. Did Jesus not say, "If you've seen Me, you've seen your Father?" You know what I am like through Christ - trustable and approachable. The world says, "save yourself, protect yourself, defend yourself" but I say surrender yourself totally to Me. Not just ankle deep, knee deep, or waist deep, but all the way in."

Today's Scriptures:

John 14:9 – Jesus said to him, "Have I been with you so long, and yet you have not known Me, Philip? He who has seen Me has seen the Father."

Isaiah 41:10 – "Fear not, for I am with you; Be not dismayed, for I am your God. I will strengthen you, Yes, I will help you, I will uphold you with My righteous right hand."

Day 94 - Raised In Christ

"Put on the new man this day. Created in righteousness and true holiness. Even as I have risen -- I have resurrected you. I have made you new. Look not to the former things, they don't define you. Look to the new you, the true you -- washed clean by My own blood, rendered innocent, wrapped in My authority, sincere, secure, and humble. Do not doubt who I have made you, only believe. Do not doubt your significance to Me, nor My kingdom work."

Today's Scriptures:

Isaiah 43:18-19 – *"Do not remember the former things, Nor consider the things of old. [19] Behold, I will do a new thing, Now it shall spring forth; Shall you not know it?"*

Romans 6:4 – *Therefore we were buried with Him through baptism into death, that just as Christ was raised from the dead by the glory of the Father, even so we also should walk in newness of life.*

Day 95 - Back To Simplicity

"Arise, My love. Do not be held by your past but be held by My glory. Fix your eyes upon Me and not your mistakes or the mistakes of others. Today, because you have humbled yourself, I lift you above the weight of circumstances. I draw you back to the intimacy, sincerity, and simplicity of walking with Me. Live by relaxed receptivity. If you can receive you can live. Relaxed receptivity is embracing the gift of God at all times."

Today's Scriptures:

2 Corinthians 11:3 – *But I fear, lest somehow, as the serpent deceived Eve by his craftiness, so your minds may be corrupted from the simplicity that is in Christ.*

Colossians 2:6-7 – *As you have therefore received Christ Jesus the Lord, so walk in Him, ⁷ rooted and built up in Him and established in the faith, as you have been taught, abounding in it with thanksgiving.*

Day 96 - God's Perspective

"I am your Vision. I am your master Light through which you can see. You do not find grace and power in the eyes of others but in the eyes of the Lord. It is MY perspective that gives you Life. It is MY view and opinion that empowers you; not what others think. What is the greater reality? What they think they see in you or what I, the One who made you, says about you? Grab peace this day, grab confidence this day-- knowing the Holy Spirit; your Teacher, Comforter, Guide, and Helper gives you eyes to see what the real truth and reality is."

Today's Scriptures:

Genesis 6:8 – *Noah found grace in the eyes of the Lord.*

Luke 11:13 – *"If you then, being evil, know how to give good gifts to your children, how much more will your heavenly Father give the Holy Spirit to those who ask Him!"*

Day 97 - Your Divine Design

"Lay down your life and take up Mine. Embrace who I've made you to be. It's My good pleasure to give you the Kingdom and all its keys. There is no other pattern for you than the one I have chosen – destined to be conformed to My image. In My eyes you see your destiny. In My eyes you see the kindness I made you for. The love I made you for. The overcoming I made you for. Rise above the enemy's whispers, embrace your design, cling to what is good."

Today's Scriptures:

Romans 8:29 – *For whom He foreknew, He also predestined to be conformed to the image of His Son, that He might be the firstborn among many brethren.*

Luke 12:32 – *"Do not fear, little flock, for it is your Father's good pleasure to give you the kingdom."*

Day 98 - Be Encouraged

"Head up, My child. Turn your face to Me, for I am your glory and the lifter of your head. Where the enemy has tried to downcast you, I am upholding you with My strong right hand. Where the enemy has tried to constrain you, I am setting you at liberty. Where the enemy has tried to cause you grief and worry, I am your Peace. This day I give you beauty for ashes, the oil of joy for mourning, the garment of praise over any spirits of heaviness. Rise up, walk in Truth, and let's manifest excellence together."

Today's Scriptures:

Isaiah 41:10 – *"Fear not, for I am with you; Be not dismayed, for I am your God. I will strengthen you, Yes, I will help you, I will uphold you with My righteous right hand."*

Isaiah 61:3 (NLT) – *To all who mourn in Israel, He will give a crown of beauty for ashes, a joyous blessing instead of mourning, festive praise instead of despair.*

Day 99 - Selfless Love

"Love is the key; not love like the world, but the love you have found in Me. Love that gives, not takes. Love that values people and what is right over license and liberty. Love that is not self-serving. The very reason I did not release My Spirit in full measure until after the cross was so you could see what love in My Spirit really is -- selfless. Love is patient. Love is kind. It does not demand its own way. It covers a multitude of sin. My love never fails. I have given you a new heart, My heart, with new desires and new motives."

Today's Scriptures:

Ezekiel 36:25-27 – *"Then I will sprinkle clean water on you, and you shall be clean; I will cleanse you from all your filthiness and from all your idols. ²⁶ I will give you a new heart and put a new spirit within you; I will take the heart of stone out of your flesh and give you a heart of flesh. ²⁷ I will put My Spirit within you and cause you to walk in My statutes."*

Day 100 - Your New History

"I am your supply for love, joy, peace, approval, and fulfillment. I am cutting off what you've been feeding on in the world that you may feed more on Me. Generational curses are broken off of you because when you were born into My family I gave you a whole new history and a whole new family tree. You are not who you once were. You are not subject to hereditary dysfunction because of what I have passed down to you-- My Life, My blood, My health. You've been washed, cleansed, sanctified, and justified. You are My dwelling place. You house My very Spirit."

Today's Scriptures:

1 Corinthians 3:16 – Do you not know that you are the temple of God and that the Spirit of God dwells in you?

2 Corinthians 6:18 – "I will be a Father to you, And you shall be My sons and daughters," says the Lord Almighty.

Day 101 - True Riches

"Come unto Me, My beloved. For this day I adorn you with a heart of thanksgiving and an attitude of gratitude. In all things give thanks, for this is My will for you in Christ Jesus. Set your mind not on the things you do not have, but on those things you do have. Whatever is pure, whatever is lovely, whatever is just and true and worthy of praise -- think on these things. Walk in the true riches of My Spirit and Kingdom, not the materialism of this world. For true riches are the things worth far more than money. True riches satisfy your soul and bring your heart contentment far more than this worlds need and greed."

Today's Scriptures:

1 Thessalonians 5:16-18 – *Rejoice always,* [17] *pray without ceasing,* [18] *in everything give thanks; for this is the will of God in Christ Jesus for you.*

Day 102 - Only Believe

"Take My hand, walk with Me. Today our focus is belief; not mere intellectual head knowledge but deep conviction of the heart. For it is true belief that affects and influences behavior. I stir within you this day belief that I am good. Belief that I am who I say I am. Belief that I am full of mercy, slow to anger and rich in love. Belief heightens you, lifts you, encourages you. Why? I made and designed you for belief. Guard against spirits of skepticism and criticism. Let your heart believe again-- soar with Me for I am joy to your soul, life to your body, and strength to your bones."

Today's Scriptures:

Hebrews 11:1 – Now faith is the substance of things hoped for, the evidence of things not seen.

Hebrews 11:6 – But without faith it is impossible to please Him, for he who comes to God must believe that He is, and that He is a rewarder of those who diligently seek Him.

Day 103 - Intimacy with Christ

"Rest as you breathe Me in. Once again I have shown you My peace is real. Once again I have demonstrated My hand upon your life. All that warfare was just the noise of your enemy trying to prevent everything I have in store for you, but he could not. You have always been safe in Me, but now you are coming to comprehend it. You have always been encircled by the depths of My love, but now you are realizing it. Look to Me and live. Be bold, be brave, and be strong in the knowledge that I am your forever Friend."

Today's Scriptures:

Joshua 1:9 (AMP) – *"Have I not commanded you? Be strong and courageous! Do not be terrified or dismayed (intimidated), for the Lord your God is with you wherever you go."*

Psalm 34:19 (KJV) – *Many are the afflictions of the righteous: but the LORD delivereth him out of them all.*

Day 104 - Becoming Peace

"Faith. Authority. Confidence. All these have been stirred in you as you take your rightful place in My plans and purposes. My power, presence, and peace have taken much deeper root in you. Those things that at one time used to own you don't even have a voice anymore. Fear, worry, anxiety; the wrong opinions of others -- do not influence you nearly as they once did. You are no longer looking for peace, you are becoming peace - every step, every word, every thought, in every situation."

Today's Scriptures:

Isaiah 26:3 – *You will keep him in perfect peace, whose mind is stayed on You, because he trusts in You.*

Romans 5:1 – *Therefore, having been justified by faith, we have peace with God through our Lord Jesus Christ.*

Day 105 - Inwardly Sourced

"Come forth, My love. Allow Me to fill you fresh with all you need. Allow Me to set your mind and be your Source so you aren't caught depending on a set of "right circumstances" to have a good day. You are not externally driven, you are internally sourced. You are not looking for peace, you are a carrier of peace. Do not underestimate your enemy. He has tested you for weaknesses but he is an already defeated foe! He has nothing on you because of My blood. Continue to lift My vision higher. Yes, as you mature there is greater resistance, but you also grow in greater authority."

Today's Scriptures:

2 Thessalonians 3:3 – _But the Lord is faithful, who will establish you and guard you from the evil one._

Colossians 1:27 – _To them God willed to make known what are the riches of the glory of this mystery among the Gentiles: which is Christ in you, the hope of glory._

Day 106 - Your Value

"Hear Me, oh child. For I desire truth in your inward parts. Truth that protects you from deception. Truth that roots and grounds you. Truth that keeps your heart from seeing yourself as less than I see you. Do I not see and know your worth? Life is not an experiment and you are most certainly not random. My love fashioned you and My purpose required your existence. Stand free and fast this day."

Today's Scriptures:

Psalm 51:6 (KJV) – Behold, thou desirest truth in the inward parts: and in the hidden part thou shalt make me to know wisdom.

Ephesians 3:17-19 - That Christ may dwell in your hearts through faith; that you, being rooted and grounded in love, [18] may be able to comprehend with all the saints what is the width and length and depth and height—[19] to know the love of Christ which passes knowledge; that you may be filled with all the fullness of God.

Day 107 - Abide In Christ

"Pause and take time in My Presence. Rest and trust My inner workings. Know My majesty and great love for you. I hold the universe in my hand and yet I formed you with detail in your mother's womb. I flung every star and yet I numbered the very hairs on your head. Abide in My Spirit and live in the dimension that sources you. Fish abide in water because water gives life to the fish. Plants abide in soil because soil gives life to the plants. Choose to abide in My Spirit because I am life to you. Good seed plus good soil in your heart always equals good fruit."

Today's Scriptures:

John 15:4-5 – "Abide in Me, and I in you. As the branch cannot bear fruit of itself, unless it abides in the vine, neither can you, unless you abide in Me ⁵ *"I am the vine, you are the branches. He who abides in Me, and I in him, bears much fruit; for without Me you can do nothing."*

Day 108 - The Truth

"Truth. Truth. I'm anchoring you in truth. Emotions are often not a proper reflection of reality. Feelings seldom are. The truth is your anchor and stability in any storm. The truth is I am with you always. The truth is I am in you to do My good pleasure. The truth is you do not have to know rejection from others because you know My acceptance. The truth is you are not susceptible to worry because you know My perfect love. You do not live from experience to experience or emotion to emotion but from truth to truth. I have no greater joy than for My children to walk in truth."

Today's Scriptures:

3 John 1:3-4 – *For I rejoiced greatly when brethren came and testified of the truth that is in you, just as you walk in the truth. ⁴ I have no greater joy than to hear that my children walk in truth.*

Day 109 - Mastered By Christ

"Whatever is true. Whatever is pure. Whatever is worthy of praise, think on these things. For whatever has your attention has you. Today we are recapturing the areas of your heart and mind that deal with belief. For as you believe in your heart so you will be. Yes, there are clouds but there is ample sunshine. Yes, you have emotions but you are not ruled by your emotions; you are ruled by truth. Because you are rooted and grounded in love, truth will always triumph over your feelings. The best way to master your circumstances is to be mastered by Me."

Today's Scripture:

Philippians 4:8 – Finally, brethren, whatever things are true, whatever things are noble, whatever things are just, whatever things are pure, whatever things are lovely, whatever things are of good report, if there is any virtue and if there is anything praiseworthy--meditate on these things.

Day 110 - Radiant Health

"Rest. Rest in My arms. Let Me love you into loving and forgive you into forgiving. For a healthy mind leads to a healthy body. Allow Me to cleanse you of any fear, worry, or strife. Allow Me to keep your mind free from meaningless speculations. For if I hold worlds together by My hand, I can hold you together and keep you. I can be your strength, your strong tower, your shield. For in Me there is radiant health-- mental, physical, emotional. You are too great a creation to be satisfied by anything but Me."

Today's Scriptures:

2 Corinthians 10:5 (NIV) – We demolish arguments and every pretension that sets itself up against the knowledge of God, and we take captive every thought to be obedient to Christ.

Hebrews 12:15 – Looking carefully lest anyone fall short of the grace of God; lest any root of bitterness spring up causing trouble, and by this many become defiled.

Day 111 - One Hope

"Come unto Me and take the hand of hope. A man can live for days without food but he can't live a day without hope. Why do so many struggle? Why are so many downcast? They have looked to the world, to politicians, to man-made systems and governments; they've even been taught to look to themselves. Yet who can supply what is needed but the Everlasting, the Creator of all, and the Prince of Peace? Take My hand and let hope live again -- in your heart, in your mind, in your song, and in your smile."

Today's Scriptures:

Romans 15:13 – May the God of hope fill you with all joy and peace as you trust in him, so that you may overflow with hope by the power of the Holy Spirit.

Psalm 71:5 – For You are my hope, O Lord God; You are my trust from my youth.

Day 112 - God Is Personal

"Awaken unto Me as I am infinitely personal. I didn't just say I love you in a book or a letter but in a Life. In the flesh and blood of My Son. In the whispers of My Voice. I welcome you to our secret place to meet together. You in Me and I in you. Growth occurs as you continue to walk in humility, intimacy, and dependence on Me. You mature as you listen to the Voice that says good things about you. For I know you better than you know yourself. I formed you. Designed you to need not just the air of this world but the breath of My Spirit."

Today's Scriptures:

John 1:14 – And the Word became flesh and dwelt among us, and we beheld His glory, the glory as of the only begotten of the Father, full of grace and truth.

John 3:16 – "For God so loved the world that He gave His only begotten Son, that whoever believes in Him should not perish but have everlasting life."

Day 113 - Your Anchor

"Rise and sing as I awaken you to this day. Walk with Me as I lead you in the paths of righteousness for My name's sake. Allow Me to navigate you through the ups and downs of life, for I am your Father. I am your Strength and Song. I am your Stability and Consistency. I am your ever present help in time of trouble. Lean into Me and My resources. For Blessed is the person who knows they've been made right by what I have done for them rather than what they've done for Me."

Today's Scriptures:

Psalm 46:1 – God is our Refuge and Strength, a very present help in trouble.

Psalm 33:12 – Blessed is the nation whose God is the Lord, the people He has chosen as His own inheritance.

Ephesians 3:16 - That He would grant you, according to the riches of His glory, to be strengthened with might through His Spirit in your inner man.

Day 114 - Everlasting Love

"Take My hand. Walk with Me. You are clean because of the word I have spoken over you. If I am not willing to remember your transgressions, why would you? For I have loved you with an everlasting love and drawn you with My loving kindness. I have numbered each of your days before there was even one of them. Let Me whisper your value, worth, and significance to you -- strengthening you, heightening you, and empowering you for this day."

Today's Scriptures:

Jeremiah 31:3 – The Lord has appeared of old to me, saying: "Yes, I have loved you with an everlasting love; therefore with loving-kindness I have drawn you."

Hebrews 8:12 – "For I will be merciful to their unrighteousness, and their sins and lawless deeds I will remember no more."

Day 115 - Joy As Strength

"Joy! Joy! My joy is your strength. Not joy from the world or your circumstances. Joy from My Spirit. Joy from the well spring of Life within you. Joy from My Presence, My peace, My perspective, My point of view. Is everything not useable? Not redeemable? How many times have I made a beautiful diamond out of what you thought was only a dark lump of coal? Beginning with the day I began reshaping you after I plucked you out of darkness."

Today's Scriptures:

Psalm 126:5-6 – Those who sow in tears Shall reap in joy. ⁶ He who continually goes forth weeping, gathering seed for sowing, Shall doubtless come again with rejoicing, Bringing his sheaves with him.

John 15:11 – "These things I have spoken to you, that My joy might remain in you and that your joy might be full."

Day 116 - Be Still And Know

"Rest, reflect, and pause. Be still and know that I am God. Be still and know how much I care for you. Be still and know I have given Myself for you. For you are flesh of My flesh and bone of My bone. You are breath of My breath and spirit of My Spirit. I made you for Myself; to know Me intra-personally. I have never asked you to earn My love, only to reflect it to those around you. I am the Vine and you are the branch. Apart from Me you can do nothing."

Today's Scriptures:

Psalm 46:10 – *"Be still and know that I am God; I will be exalted among the nations, I will be exalted in the Earth!"*

John 17:3 – *"And this is eternal life, that they may know you, the only true God, and Jesus Christ whom you have sent."*

1 Corinthians 6:17 – *But he who is joined to the Lord is one spirit with Him.*

Day 117 - Made Clean

"Come. Come to Me. I have not left you. I have not abandoned you. I am not even capable of that. I am with you always even until the end of the age. Do you think I don't understand your humanness? That I somehow don't understand your weakness? I became flesh. I have been touched with the very feeling of your infirmity, tempted in every way, yet without sin. Look to Me. Let me remind you of the truth of who and whose you are. Do not call unclean that which I have made clean-- you."

Today's Scriptures:

Hebrews 4:15-16 – For we do not have a High Priest who cannot sympathize with our weaknesses, but was in all points tempted as we are, yet without sin. [16] Let us therefore come boldly to the throne of grace, that we may obtain mercy and find grace to help in the time of need.

3 John 1:4 - I have no greater joy than to hear that my children walk in truth.

Day 118 - God's Grace

"Raise your eyes to Me. For I am your glory and the lifter of your head. No shame or guilt can keep you down. I will not allow it. I am your restart and reboot button. It is written, "If any man be in Christ, old things have passed away, behold new things have come." It is also written, "My mercies are new every morning." Take My hand, let us do right today, not SO you'll be right with Me, but because you are right with Me. My grace IS sufficient for you. My grace sought you, My grace bought you, My grace taught you, My grace caught you."

Today's Scriptures:

1 Corinthians 15:10 – But by the grace of God I am what I am, and His grace toward me was not in vain; but I labored more abundantly than they all, yet not I, but the grace of God which was with me.

Romans 3:24 (NIV) – All are justified freely by His grace through the redemption that came by Christ Jesus.

Day 119 - Redemptive Hands

"Trust in Me. Trust My redeeming power. Wait for the end result. For how many times have I turned what the enemy meant for your harm into something that benefited you? The mountains we have climbed gave you greater endurance. The obstacles we lifted simply made you stronger. Even the tears you cried I used to put seed in your hand to help so many others. There is nothing I can't turn. There is nothing I can't use. Put every experience in My redemptive hands for I waste nothing!"

Today's Scriptures:

Luke 21:12-13 – *"But before all these things, they will lay their hands on you and persecute you, delivering you up to the synagogues and prisons. You will be brought before kings and rulers for My names sake. 13 But it will turn out for you as an occasion for testimony."*

Psalm 27:8 - *When You said, "Seek My face," my heart said to You, "Your face, Lord, I will seek."*

Day 120 - Be Thankful

"Embrace Me, embrace thankfulness. Guard your grateful heart. It is such a strength to you. Guard your attitude of gratitude. Many times your enemy comes to steal it from you as he did the prodigal's older brother, who couldn't see all that I had was his. He wants your eyes on the things you do not have in order to rob you of the blessedness of the things you do. Look unto Me -- I am your Provider, your Keeper, and your Sustainer. I am the secret to the contentment that evades so many."

Today's Scriptures:

Psalm 107:1-2 – Oh give thanks to the Lord for He is good! For His mercy endures forever. ² Let the redeemed of the Lord say so, whom He has redeemed from the hand of the enemy.

1 Thessalonians 5:18 – In everything give thanks; for this is the will of God in Christ Jesus for you.

Day 121 - God's Spirit

"Arise My love. Breathe deeply My breath. For the same power and Spirit that raised Christ from the dead lives in you. Can it not also overcome your griefs and fears? Can it not also give life and health to your body that houses it? I tell you truly it can. You have power by My Spirit. You have authority by My Spirit. It is life to you. It is health to you. Let My Spirit be the words in your mouth and empower you to strengthen those around you."

Today's Scriptures:

Romans 8:11 (NLT) – *The Spirit of God, who raised Jesus from the dead, lives in you. And just as God raised Christ Jesus from the dead, He will give life to your mortal bodies by the same Spirit living in you.*

Ezekiel 37:10 – *So I prophesied as He commanded me, and breath came into them, and they lived, and stood up on their feet an exceedingly great army.*

Day 122 - Come Away

"Come, come away with Me. Away from the noise, away from the busyness-- to the stillness of My voice and the quiet strength of My Spirit. Meditation is medication. Meditate on Me, meditate on My words, for I have sent them to heal you. Softly and tenderly I call to you and to your heart. Incline your ear to my sayings; do not let them depart from your eyes. Keep them in the midst of your heart; for they are life to your soul and health to your body."

Today's Scriptures:

Proverbs 4:20-23 (NLT) – My child, pay attention to what I say. Listen carefully to My words. 21 Don't lose sight of them. Let them penetrate deep into your heart, 22 For they bring life to those who find them and healing to their whole body. 23 Guard your heart above all else, for it determines the course of your life.

Psalm 107:20 – He sent His word and healed them, and delivered them from their destructions.

Day 123 - Fruit Bearing

"I am your Vine. You are My branch. Therefore fruit does not come FROM you, fruit comes THROUGH you. Fruit is not the basis of our relationship, it's the byproduct of it. I ask for your heart to simply be willing to receive from Me on a daily basis. If you will but receive, you will know My supply, and because you know My supply, you will never lack for anything. You will never be short on love. Never be short on joy. Never be short on peace. I am your Vine. Simply abide in Me."

Today's Scriptures:

John 15:4-5 (NLT) – *"Remain in Me, and I will remain in you. For a branch cannot produce fruit if it is severed from the vine, and you cannot be fruitful unless you remain in Me. 5 Yes, I am the Vine; you are the branches. Those who remain in Me and I in them will produce much fruit. For apart from Me you can do nothing."*

Day 124 - Divine Health

"Rise into life, peace, and health. For more than I desire granting you periodic miracles of healing, I desire you to walk in divine health each day. For everything I taught you through Christ -- every principle, attitude, and command was life giving and health producing. Forgiveness, kindness, understanding, patience, humility, love, mercy, and compassion are all health to the human mind, body, and spirit; whereas bitterness, vengeance, malice, anger, and hatred are not. Do not over emphasize the miraculous and miss My plan for living daily in divine health. Rise and be whole."

Today's Scriptures:

3 John 1:2 – *Beloved I pray that you may prosper in all things and be in health, even as your soul prospers.*

1 Peter 2:24 – *Himself bore our sins in His own body on the tree, that we, having died to sins, might live for righteousness- by whose stripes you were healed.*

Day 125 - True Government

"Rest in Me as I rest in you. Enjoy My Presence as it conforms you to the image of My Son. Let Me fill you and remind you of your purity, meekness, and righteousness in Me. Pray for the nation. Pray people see through the bickering and strife the enemy creates. Pray they humble themselves and remember the real hope for America is My Spirit living triumphantly in and through the human heart. That is the greatest form of government ever -- for it transforms the inside, the motive, the nature of a man. No policy, no legislation can do that; and that is where the nation is broken, on the inside."

Today's Scriptures:

1 Peter 5:6 – Therefore humble yourselves under the mighty hand of God, that He may exalt you in due time.

Isaiah 9:6 – For unto us a child is born, unto us a Son is given; and the government will be upon His shoulder.

Day 126 - Divine Health

"Awake, My love. Trust wholeheartedly in Me. For do you not know that because of your new birth, My blood now flows through your veins? My purity has become your purity. My righteousness has become yours. My very Life and Spirit are in you bringing healing and health to your mortal body. Is there anything impossible? Is there anything we cannot touch redemptively together? If I be for you who can be against you? Trust and be not afraid. Embrace what I have done in you. Be who I've made you to be, not who others try to condition you to be."

Today's Scriptures:

Romans 8:31 – What then shall we say to these things? If God is for us, who can be against us?

Romans 8:11 (TLB) – And the Spirit of God, who raised up Jesus from the dead, lives in you, He will make your dying bodies live again after you die, by means of the same Holy Spirit living within you.

Day 127 - Loving Others

"My precious child. My love is sufficient for you. My love is more than enough for you. For only My love can satisfy. Loving others from a place of neediness, for what they can give you in return, isn't love at all; it actually reveals you have believed a lie that you lack for something. I've not taught you love in that way. Love from a place of abundance, of overflow, of being given, of being surrendered – live full and love from the depths of My love for you, for that is genuine."

Today's Scriptures:

1 John 4:19 – We love Him because He first loved us.

John 7:38 – "He who believes in Me, as the Scripture has said, out of his heart will flow rivers of living water."

John 15:9 – "As the Father loved Me, I also have loved you; abide in My love."

Day 128 - Leading Others

"Come forth My love, for your past no longer has a hold on you. Listen for the song of My heart. Feel the presence of My hand in yours - leading you, guiding you. For will I ever leave you or forsake you? I tell you truly I am incapable of that. I am forever faithful. I am forever yours. I am forever committed to your growth and development. Today I give you grace to live out what I have asked of you-- to be a blessing, to be a giver not a taker, a mentor, a leader, someone given to heightening those around you."

Today's Scripture:

Acts 20:35 (NLT) – _And I have been a constant example of how you can help those in need by working hard. You should remember the words of the Lord Jesus: "It is more blessed to give than to receive."_

Matthew 20:28 – _"Just as the Son of Man did not come to be served, but to serve, and to give His life a ransom for many."_

Day 129 - Your Significance

"Embrace My truth. Align with Me. Let Me take your eyes off of others and put them on who you are, the grace I've given you, the gifts inside you, and what I've called you to do and be. Jealousy and comparing yourself with others has no place in you. Am I not the Divine Orchestrator who orders your steps? Trust in Me and believe how valuable and significant I Myself have made you. Live confidently before Me. You know who you are and you know whose you are."

Today's Scriptures:

2 Corinthians 10:12 – For we dare not class ourselves or compare ourselves with those who commend themselves. But they, measuring themselves by themselves, and comparing themselves among themselves, are not wise.

John 21:22 – And Jesus said, "If I will that he remain until I come, what is that to you? You follow Me."

Day 130 - God's Workmanship

"Bless those who try to hurt you, pray for those who try to use you. I tell you do not overcome evil with evil but overcome evil with good - so proving that I am your Source for life, love, and peace-- not the actions or attitudes of others. If you think you are who you are because of someone else, that renders you a victim and powerless. Instead, you are who you are because I made you who you are. You are strong in My strength, valued in My value, and accepted in My acceptance."

Today's Scriptures:

Matthew 5:46-48 – *"For if you love those who love you, what reward have you? Do not even the tax collectors do the same? 47 And if you greet your brethren only, what do you do more than others? Do not even the tax collectors do so? 48 Therefore you shall be perfect, just as your Father in heaven is perfect."*

Day 131 - Rise Up

"Be renewed and refreshed this day. Yes, you have made mistakes but they cannot hold you down. Why? You do not serve your past, your past serves you. For do I not use even your failures to grow you and teach you? To show you how My character does not waiver with your behavior. I tell you truly everything is usable to Me. I waste nothing. Your tests become your testimonies. Your messes become your messages. I am your invincibility. Rise up once again this day and be who I say you are."

Today's Scriptures:

Proverbs 24:16 (NIV) – For though a righteous man falls seven times, he rises again.

Psalm 103:12 – As far as the east is from the west, so far has He removed our transgressions from us.

Luke 9:56 – "For the Son of Man did not come to destroy men's lives but to save them."

Day 132 - A New Name

"Behold I have changed your name. You are no longer called barren or forsaken; but I have called you fruitful, forgiven, free, and fulfilled. Is there anything too difficult for Me? My purpose summoned your very existence. I set you at the right place in time just as I did Moses, Paul, Abraham and others. You are blessed-- and blessed to be a blessing. I tell you truly nothing can separate you from My love; not principalities nor powers, not things past nor present nor things to come. Know and believe the love I have for you."

Today's Scripture:

Genesis 28:14 (NIV) – *Your descendants will be like the dust of the earth, and you will spread out to the west and to the east, to the north and to the south. All peoples on earth will be blessed through you and your offspring.*

1 John 4:16 – *And we have known and believed the love God has for us.*

Day 133 - A Victorious Life

"Rest in Me My child, for the wind and waves still know My Name. You are not a victim regardless of the actions of others around you because I have made you victorious. I can take whatever the enemy means for evil and bring good out of it; even gold out of it, that empowers you and brings healing to others. You are therefore invincible in Me for you can not only overcome everything that happens to you, you can USE everything that happens to you for good."

Today's Scriptures:

Romans 8:28 (NIV) – *And we know that in all things God works for the good of those who love Him, who have been called according to His purpose.*

Matthew 4:39 – *Then He arose and rebuked the wind, and said to the sea, "Peace, be still!" And the wind ceased and there was a great calm.*

Day 134 - Forgiveness Heals

"Peace be still. Trust in My Word. Do not forgive because your salvation is at risk, forgive because your health and peace of mind are. For forgiveness heals two ways: when you receive it AND when you give it. Forgiveness is an opportunity for you to share with others what I have generously shared with you – patience, and understanding. Past wounds move from an obstacle to an opportunity when you understand the power of My forgiveness."

Today's Scriptures:

1 John 2:12 (NIV) – I am writing to you, dear children, because your sins have been forgiven on account of his name.

Hebrews 10:17-18 – Then He adds, "Their sins and their lawless deeds I will remember no more." [18] Now where there is remission of these, there is no longer an offering for sin.

Day 135 - Changing The World

"Be stilled and be filled. Pause and reflect on all I have done out of My love for you and for all of humanity. If you think I didn't enter the world to change the world you missed the meaning of My coming. I sowed peace into the world that I might reap peace in the world. I sowed love into the world that I might reap love in the world. I sowed goodwill that I might reap goodwill. Knowing fully that man was never capable of extending peace, love, and goodwill until He had first witnessed it from Me."

Today's Scriptures:

Luke 2:14 (KJV) – Glory to God in the highest, and on earth peace, good will toward men.

John 12:24 (NLT) – "I tell you the truth, unless a kernel of wheat is planted in the soil and dies, it remains alone. But its death will produce many new kernels--a plentiful harvest of new lives."

Day 136 - Humility And Rest

"Remain calm, My child. No need to push your own agenda through. For it is written, "Love never demands its own way." How often has one demanded his own way and then not been able to enjoy what he demanded? Humility, rest, and intimacy are such keys to the high life of My kingdom. Stand, set your mind on Me; I protect it with My peace and will do great things in and through you."

Today's Scriptures:

Hebrews 4:3 (NLT) – For only we who believe can enter His rest.

1 Corinthians 13:4-5 – Love suffers long and is kind; love does not envy; love does not parade itself, is not puffed up; 5 does not behave rudely, does not seek its own, is not provoked, thinks no evil.

Isaiah 26:3 – You will keep him in perfect peace, whose mind is stayed on You.

Day 137 - Power Of Love

"Stop. Rest. Listen. Take time to listen to the Voice that says good things about you. For I speak life and peace to My people. Do I see the violence? Yes, I do. Do I see the hatred born out of deception? Yes, I do. Do I see the turning a blind eye? Yes, I do. But again I say, walk by the Spirit. Walk in truth despite what others do or say. Live by My Presence, not by performance. You be you. The power of love will always conquer the love of power, for My love never fails. Hatred is an already defeated foe operating on ever diminishing returns."

Today's Scriptures:

Psalm 85:8 (NLT) – I listen carefully to what God the LORD is saying, for He speaks peace to His faithful people. But let them not return to their foolish ways.

Galatians 5:16 – But I say, walk by the Spirit, and you will not carry out the desire of the flesh.

Day 138 - God Is Faithful

"My accepted child. Contrary to what your enemy says, I am not far from you, I am both with you and in you -- there to will and to do My good pleasure. There to never leave you nor forsake you. There to be a friend that sticks closer than a brother. First I gathered you, then I cleansed you, then I gave you a new heart, and then I put My very Spirit inside you; that from there I may forever teach you who we are together."

Today's Scriptures:

Philippians 2:13 (KJV) – For it is God which worketh in you both to will and to do of His good pleasure.

John 14:17 – "The Spirit of Truth, whom the world cannot receive, because it neither sees Him or knows Him; but you know Him, for He dwells with you and will be in you."

Day 139 - Triumphant Faith

"Beloved, meet the day in triumphant faith. For it is written, "This is the victory that overcomes the world, even our faith." Yes, there are trials, yes, there are frustrations; but be of good cheer I have overcome the natural world for you. I have stripped it of its power to overtake you. Flee worry and anxiety, they are not of Me. Remember, the things you worry about rarely turn out to be as harmful as the worry itself."

Today's Scriptures:

John 16:33 (New AMP) – *"I have told you these things, so that in Me you may have [perfect] peace. In the world you have tribulation and distress and suffering, but be courageous [be confident, be undaunted, be filled with joy]; I have overcome the world." [My conquest is accomplished, My victory abiding.]*

1 John 5:4 – *This is the victory that overcomes the world, even our faith.*

Day 140 - Clear Vision

"Let Me wash your mind and your vision as I restore and refresh you. It's time for clear eyes, renewed thoughts, and renewed perspective -- My perspective. For My perspective is clear of all the world's clutter. What have I ever wrung My hands over? As you align your mind with My Word and as you align your eyes with My view; your attitude is heightened, your day is brightened, your understanding enlightened. What is said of those who possess a pure heart? They shall see God."

Today's Scriptures:

Revelation 3:18 – _"I counsel you to buy from Me gold refined in the fire, that you may be rich; and white garments, that you may be clothed, that the shame of your nakedness may not be revealed; and anoint your eyes with eye salve, that you may see."_

Proverbs 29:18 – _Where there is no vision, the people perish._

Day 141 - Loving Others

"Oh My child, if you could just see what I see in you. Truly you are worth more than you have been told; you can do more than what you've believed. I love using YOU to show My love to others. I love using YOU to touch others, to heal others, to encourage those who are troubled and down. Yes, I could do it all on My own, but I have chosen instead to do those things through people like you. Just as I sent the first body of Christ to touch and heal, I desire to use the current body of Christ to do the same."

Today's Scriptures:

John 14:12 – "Most assuredly, I say to you, he who believes in Me, the works that I do he will do also; and greater works than these he will do, because I go to My Father."

Matthew 10:1 – When He had called His twelve disciples to Him, He gave them power over unclean spirits, to cast them out, and to heal all kinds of sickness and all kinds of disease.

Day 142 - Who's Keeping You

"Do not entertain the lies and whispers of your enemy. Who you were in your past is NOT greater than who you are in your present. Trust in Me and be not afraid. Watch and see ~ for I will take you and make you outwardly all that I say you are inwardly. Know that I am keeping you, sustaining you. For until you know who's keeping you, you'll look to everyone else to keep you -- Keep you happy, keep you valuable, keep you going."

Today's Scriptures:

John 10:10 – *"The thief does not come except to steal, and to kill, and to destroy. I have come that they may have life, and that they may have it more abundantly."*

Isaiah 43:18-19 – *Do not remember the former things, nor consider the things of old. 19 Behold, I will do a new thing, Now it shall spring forth; Shall you not know it? I will even make a road in the wilderness And rivers in the desert.*

Day 143 - Christ As Source

"I am your Supply. Live from Me not your own resources. You love because I first loved you. You forgive because I first forgave you. You offer peace because I first offered it to you. Do not live like you are earning something from Me; live like you have already received something from Me. What a blessing to serve others because you are full and you genuinely care for them; not so you can "earn something" or "get something." When you received of My Breath and Spirit, you received all that pertains to life and Godliness."

Today's Scriptures:

2 Peter 1:3 (NIV) – *His divine power has given us everything we need for a godly life through our knowledge of Him who called us by His own glory and goodness.*

Romans 5:1 (NIV) – *Therefore, since we have been justified through faith, we have peace with God through our Lord Jesus Christ.*

Day 144 - Embrace Dependence

"Trust and be not afraid. I have no condemnation for you, in fact I have set you free from all condemnation and accusation. Instead allow your weakness to drive you to reliance upon Me. This is the Christian life, Me living and loving through you daily. You have a treasure yes, but in an earthen vessel -- that the power revealed in you would be known to be from Me. Weakness teaches you dependence. Weakness teaches you humility. I have joined together human weakness and My strength. What I have joined together let no man separate. For when you are weak, then I AM STRONG."

Today's Scriptures:

Romans 8:1-2 – *There is therefore now no condemnation for those who are in Christ. 2 For the law of the Spirit of life in Christ Jesus has made me free from the law of sin and death.*

Joel 3:10 – *Let the weak say, "I am strong!"*

Day 145 - God is Here

"Quiet your mind and realize - I am here. Take a deep breath and realize - I am here. My love is here. Like ocean waves upon a shore, My love is steady, faithful, and unrelenting upon you. Like steady rain on a house top, My grace covers every part of you. When you try to run, I follow you. When you try to hide, I call your name. When you feel lost, I comfort you. I am the faithful One. The everlasting One. I am the Lighthouse amidst any dark waters you may stumble into. Just quiet your mind and realize - I am here."

Today's Scriptures:

Matthew 10:29-30 – *"Are not two sparrows sold for a copper coin? And not one of them falls to the ground apart from your Father's will. 30 But the very hairs of your head are all numbered."*

Psalm 147:3 – *He heals the brokenhearted and binds up their wounds.*

Day 146 - Your True Identity

"This day lay hold of that for which I have laid hold of you. Embrace your destiny and significance in Me. Live out your true identity. No one else can name you because I've already named you. No one else can label you because I've already labeled you. You are My dwelling place. You are My dearly beloved. I have hidden you in My Son. You are never alone, never helpless, never lacking. Forget what is behind. Reach for what is ahead. Press through the opposition."

Today's Scriptures:

Philippians 3:12 – *Not that I have already attained, or am already perfected; but I press on, that I may lay hold of that for which Christ Jesus has also laid hold of me.*

Colossians 3:3 – *For you died, and your life is hidden with Christ in God.*

Day 147 - Inward Work

"You are never so much your own as when you inwardly decide to be Mine. Begin each day reaffirming that you belong to Me. More important than you having passion for Me is you knowing I have much passion for you. For you can only love others to the degree that you believe I love you. Spend time each day knowing the deep love that I have for you. A love that knows no end, that is selfless and sacrificial. Enjoy relaxed receptivity over self effort; knowing quality receptivity will always precede quality productivity."

Today's Scriptures:

John 13:34 – *"A new commandment I give to you, that you love one another; as I have loved you, that you also love one another."*

Matthew 5:3 (NEB) – *"How blest are they who know their need of God, all of Heaven is theirs."*

Day 148 - Be Whole

"Be light, be salt. Be strong in My strength. Be whole in My wholeness. There are many who need to see the graciousness, wisdom, and peace I can bring. Do not enter into the flesh with them; be hospitable, understanding, and truthful. Remember, this is warfare; not a fantasy cruise. It takes greater strength to respond right when you're being done wrong than to repay evil for evil. You possess this strength in Me. I will be the words in your mouth, I will be your wisdom."

Today's Scriptures:

Romans 12:18 – *If it is possible, as much as depends on you, live peaceably with all men.*

Matthew 5:14 – *"You are the light of the world. A city that is set on a hill cannot be hidden."*

James 3:16 (NIV) – *But the wisdom that comes from heaven is first of all pure; then peace-loving, considerate, submissive, full of mercy and good fruit, impartial and sincere.*

Day 149 - Fear Is A Facade

"Hear Me, My beloved. Fear is a facade. An already defeated foe trying to rear its ugly head. Fear is not real because it is based on the lie I won't take care of you. That you're not safe with Me. That you're not squarely in the palm of My hand, or securely centered as the apple of My eye. Flee the speculative thoughts, voices, and emotions that try to take you outside of truth. Remain steadfast, deeply embedded in the confidence that I am ordering your steps and no other."

Today's Scriptures:

Isaiah 41:13 (NIV) – "I am the Lord, your God, who takes hold of your right hand and says to you, do not fear; I will help you."

2 Kings 6:16-17 – So he answered, "Do not fear, for those who are with us are more than those who are with them." [17] And Elisha prayed, and said, "Lord, I pray, open his eyes that he may see."

Day 150 - Your Divine Design

"Lean and rely upon Me. Do not fear and do not worry; only believe. For I am the way, the truth, and the life. I am the way you are designed to live. I am the truth about you. I am the life that is to be expressed through your mortal body. Hear My Word and keep on hearing. Eat of Me and keep on eating. Drink of Me and keep on drinking. Why? Because repetition and reinforcement are such keys to your growth. Behold, I am life, health, and peace to you."

Today's Scriptures:

John 14:6 – Jesus said to him, "I am the way, the truth, and the life. No one comes to the Father except through Me."

Romans 10:17 – Faith comes by hearing and hearing by the Word of God.

John 6:54 – "Whoever eats My flesh and drinks My blood has eternal life, and I will raise him up at the last day."

Day 151 - Your Life Line

"Oh child, I hear your heart. You try and hide your face from me, yet I will never hide Mine from you. You try and hide your weaknesses from Me, yet I will never withhold My strength from you. When you found Me, you found yourself. For I am your life line, your strong tower, your Security and your Sanctuary. Nothing shall overtake you as I uphold you with My strong right hand. Nothing shall subdue you as I've made you more than a conqueror, a royal priesthood, and a holy nation."

Today's Scriptures:

1 Peter 2:9-10 (MSG) – *But you are the ones chosen by God, chosen for the high calling of priestly work, chosen to be a holy people, God's instruments to do His work and speak out for Him, to tell others of the night-and-day difference He made for you, [10] from nothing to something, from rejected to accepted.*

Day 152 - You Are Home

"Rise and breathe again. For what once constrained you is lifted. You are no longer rejected, lost, or alone. You are found, you are home, and you belong. Not only do you belong to creation and to life, but you belong to Me. And in Me everything fits. In Me everything is held together. I have called you chosen. I have called you resilient. I have called you victorious. Others have tried to count you out but back again we come. I have laid the plans before you and together we are invincible."

Today's Scriptures:

John 3:17 (MSG) – *"God didn't go to all the trouble of sending His Son merely to point an accusing finger, telling the world how bad it was. He came to help, to put the world right again."*

Hebrews 1:3 (NCV) – *The Son reflects the glory of God and shows exactly what God is like. He holds all together with His powerful word.*

Day 153 - Your Empowerment

"Awake and live. What do you have that you did not first receive? You take in, you breathe out. You receive of Me, you impart to others. What I supply to you, I invite you to embody and share. When I gave you unlimited forgiveness, I was empowering you to be a forgiving person. When I showed you unlimited mercy, I was empowering you to be a merciful person. When I made you wholly righteous, I was empowering you to put My righteousness on display for all to see. The things I get to you in the person of My Son, I desire to get through you. Do not close your heart to the truth. Do not close your mind to My thoughts. For they are health to all your flesh and strength to all your bones."

Today's Scripture:

1 Corinthians 4:7 (NIV) – For who makes you different from anyone else? What do you have that you did not receive? And if you did receive it, why do you boast as though you did not?

Day 154 - Where You Belong

"Come My child. You cannot please everyone so you may as well fix your eyes on pleasing Me. Trying to please others won't satisfy you or them in the end. So come, come away with Me, come walk with Me again. Look into My eyes and remember where you belong. I am your Source and Supply. You are a spirit being created to live in Spirit and in truth. Cease subjecting yourself to the whims and opinions of others. Come back to your first love, come home to true love. You have been left dry and thirsty, but I am here with the oil and the wine."

Today's Scriptures:

Luke 10:33-34 – *"But a certain Samaritan, as he journeyed, came where he was. And when he saw him, he had compassion. 34 So he went to him and bandaged his wounds, pouring on oil and wine; and he set him on his own animal, brought him to an inn, and took care of him."*

Day 155 - Unfailing Grace

"Come let Me lift your head once again. Let Me turn your gaze to Me where it belongs. For whatever has your attention has you. The tragedy is not that you stumbled into a sin or did something you wished you hadn't, the tragedy is that the enemy has used the shame and guilt of it to try and get you to move off the destiny I have placed within you. Who told you I would have stones and accusations for you? Never! Recall with all you are My steadfast love and unfailing grace."

Today's Scriptures:

John 8:10-11 (NLT) – *Then Jesus stood up again and said to the woman, "Where are your accusers? Didn't even one of them condemn you?" 11 "No, Lord," she said. And Jesus said, "Neither do I. Go and sin no more."*

Jeremiah 30:17 (NIV) – *"I will restore you to health and heal your wounds," says the Lord.*

Day 156 - Time To Thrive

"Arise in the Spirit once again. Now is the time. Now is the season we stand. Let us stand in truth, in right, in valor. Do not be lax, do not be passive but understand what the will of the Lord is. Possess it, wear it, become one with it that you may thrive and not just survive. For I have not called you to survival mode, but I have called you as champion, as triumphant. Your name is victory not defeat. Your name is clarity not confusion. Embrace the truth. Embrace your destiny in Me. Rise, rise, rise above the fray. Emerge this day and stand in the strength, safety, and power of My Spirit."

Today's Scriptures:

Psalm 144:1-2 (NIV) – Praise be to the LORD my Rock, who trains my hands for war, my fingers for battle. ² My lovingkindness and my fortress, my stronghold and my deliverer, my shield and He in whom I take refuge.

Day 157 - Breakthrough!

"Rejoice! Oh My child, you are on the verge of a great breakthrough. Even now the bars of iron are beginning to melt like wax at My Presence and My truth. My loves awakens over you like the morning sunrise over a calm and crystal sea. The lies of old that said you aren't safe don't hold you anymore. Those old fears of rejection leave you even now as I wrap My strong arms around you, claim you as My own, and rest you here in My arms."

Today's Scriptures:

Psalm 107:13-16 (NLT) – "LORD, help!" they cried in their trouble, and He saved them from their distress. [14] He led them from the darkness and deepest gloom; He snapped their chains. [15] Let them praise the LORD for His great love and for the wonderful things He has done for them. [16] For He broke down their prison gates of bronze; He cut apart their bars of iron.

Day 158 - Fresh Vision

"Arise with confidence as vision has found its way into your heart again. Fresh vision is in your heart because you know you are Mine. It's in your heart because you recognize the enemy's lies and that I was NEVER through with you. It's in your heart because there are so many who need who I am through you. Like a fresh wind blowing before the rain, I am blowing on you once again. Do not draw back. Stand strong in Me - undeterred, unwavering, and unshakeable."

Today's Scriptures:

Proverbs 29:18 (KJV) – *Where there is no vision, the people perish.*

Habakkuk 2:2-3 – *Then the Lord answered me and said: "Write the vision and make it plain on tablets, that he may run who reads it. ³ For the vision is yet for an appointed time; but at the end it will speak, and it will not lie. Though it tarries, wait for it; Because it will surely come, it will not tarry."*

Day 159 - Greater Measure

"Rejoice! My Spirit and My Glory are with you and in you, but is upon you in greater measure in this season. How deep will you wade out with Me? Ankle deep? Knee deep? Waist deep? Fully immersed? I speak to you, "Patience." Why be in a hurry? Will you wait upon Me? Will you allow time for Me to do things deep in your heart or will you be rushed? What can I the Lord do with a patient, trusting, willing, and humble heart? Let us find out together."

Today's Scriptures:

Isaiah 40:28-31 — *The everlasting God, the Lord, neither faints nor is weary. His understanding is unsearchable.* ²⁹ *He gives power to the weak, and to those who have no might He increases strength.* ³⁰ *Even the youth shall faint and be weary, and the young men shall utterly fall,* ³¹ *but those who wait on the Lord shall renew their strength; they will mount up with wings like eagles, they shall run and not be weary, they shall walk and not faint.*

Day 160 - What You Have

"My beloved – you experience self-control not because I've bound your hands, but because My love has bound your heart. My life and love in you, as you, and through you is all the strength you need to defeat what tempts you. I say again -- you are not trying to gain something you lack, you are expressing something you have. You are not the source of My power, you are the carrier of it. You will never live beyond your level of belief in Me and the truth I say about you. Come to Me as a needy child, and I will send you to the world as an equipped adult."

Today's Scriptures:

2 Corinthians 5:14-15 (NCV) – The love of Christ controls us, because we know that One died for all, so all have died. [15] Christ died for all so that those who live would not continue to live for themselves. He died for them and was raised from the dead so that they would live for Him.

Day 161 - God's Love

"Hear My voice call. Take heed to My words. My love will always lift you into higher living. My love is a love for all involved, not just some. My love empowers you to self-control not self-seeking. My love is not based on you, it has been placed on you. My love provides you with perspective and pure motive. My love is not conforming to the world but being transformed by a renewed mind. My love draws you to surrender to My will and My ways. My love keeps you humble. My love is not greedy or selfish; it gives, it invests, it hopes for others. My love protects. My love defends. My love is truth. My love is what all of creation needs."

Today's Scripture:

Zephaniah 3:17 (AMP) – *"The LORD your God is in your midst, a Warrior who saves. He will rejoice over you with joy; He will be quiet in His love [making no mention of your past sins], He will rejoice over you with shouts of joy."*

Day 162 - The Solution

"Listen, My child. The solution you seek is found in Me and My love for you. It runs deeper and wider than you could ever imagine. It is written, 'Perfect love casts out all fear' so LET Me love you. Let My love pour over you in wave after wave of security and stability. Join Me in vanquishing the enemies of your soul ~ fear, worry, doubt, and anxiety; replacing them with bravery, belief, peace, and confidence."

Today's Scriptures:

1 John 4:18 – *There is no fear in love; but perfect love casts out all fear, because fear involves torment. But he who fears has not been made perfect in love.*

Jeremiah 31:3 – *The Lord has appeared of old to me, saying: "Yes, I have loved you with an everlasting love; therefore with loving-kindness I have drawn you."*

Day 163 - Heart To Heart

"Welcome back My child. Welcome back to truth. For now you know I have called you. You know I have consecrated you by My holy hand. My peace is ever present with you. Your future is clear. Day by day I eradicated the fears of your past. Day by day I grew you in greater liberty, maturity, and trust. There was a time you thought days like these were out of reach, but here we are, walking together, not only hand in hand but heart to heart, in health and hope!"

Today's Scriptures:

John 17:22-23 (NIV) – _"I have given them the glory that you gave Me, that they may be one as We are one—_ [23] _I in them and You in Me—so that they may be brought to complete unity. Then the world will know that You sent Me and have loved them even as You have loved Me."_

Day 164 - God Satisfies

"Take My hand and remember who satisfies you. The pleasures of this life are fleeting, temporary, and unfulfilling. It is written that those who hunger and thirst for righteousness shall be filled and satisfied. This is because I made you FOR righteousness. Do not merely see Me, but see Me with an unveiled face. Take off any masks you have and pull down any veils, for you no longer have to change yourself. You simply become like the One which you gaze at with an unveiled face. No struggling, no trying – only looking at Me and offering your inner surrender."

Today's Scripture:

2 Corinthians 3:18 (NLT) – *So all of us who have had that veil removed can see and reflect the glory of the Lord. And the Lord—who is the Spirit—makes us more and more like Him as we are changed into His glorious image.*

Day 165 - Married To God

"Arise and awake. Be sensitive in this season to My voice. For you are stronger than you think you are. You are significant. You are marked for success by My very right hand. It is time to lay aside the residue of the old thought patterns of inadequacy and insufficiency and embrace the truth. The truth of who I've made you. I have changed your name from forsaken, fallen, and deserted to accepted, healed, gracious, beautiful, righteous, and influential. You are more than what you've thought, you are more than what you've been told. I have married you! Arise and awake!"

Today's Scriptures:

Isaiah 62:4-5 (NIV) – *"No longer will they call you deserted or desolate. but you will be called Hephzibah, and your land Beulah; for the LORD will take delight in you, and your land will be married. ⁵ As a young man marries a young woman, so will your Builder marry you; as a bridegroom rejoices over his bride, so will your God rejoice over you."*

All Scripture references are New King James
Version unless otherwise indicated:

AMP – The Amplified Bible
GNT – Good News Translation
GWT – God's Word Translation
KJV – King James Version
MSG – The Message Bible
NCV – New Century Version
NEB – New English Bible
NIV – New International Version
NLT – New Living Translation
TLB – The Living Bible